Robinson Crusoe

A Pantomime

John Morley

Samuel French - London
New York - Toronto - Hollywood

© 1983 BY JOHN MORLEY

Rights of Performance by Amateurs are controlled by Samuel French Ltd, 52 Fitzroy Street, London W1P 6JR, and they, or their authorized agents, issue licences to amateurs on payment of a fee. **It is an infringement of the Copyright to give any performance or public reading of the play before the fee has been paid and the licence issued.**

The Royalty Fee indicated below is subject to contract and subject to variation at the sole discretion of Samuel French Ltd.

Basic fee for each and every
performance by amateurs   Code K
in the British Isles

The publication of this play does not imply that it is necessarily available for performance by amateurs or professionals, either in the British Isles or Overseas. Amateurs and professionals considering a production are strongly advised in their own interests to apply to the appropriate agents for consent before starting rehearsals or booking a theatre or hall.

ISBN 0 573 06468 7

Please see page x for further copyright information.

CHARACTERS

MORTALS
Robinson Crusoe
Mrs Chrissie Crusoe, his mother
Kenny Crusoe, his brother
Captain Perkins of the *Mary Rose*
Polly Perkins, his daughter
Bill Barnacle, the bosun
Ben Dover, the mate
Blackpatch, the Pirate
Jack Boot, another pirate, his crony
Wotta Woppa, the Queen of the Cannibals
Man Friday
Old Jim, an ancient mariner
Lord Nelson
The Grunting Gorilla

IMMORTALS
Oylslick, the sea demon
Detergenta, the sea fairy

CHORUS, playing the parts of—
The Ship's Crew; Pirates; Cannibals; Demon Oylslick's Minions; and (optional) Under The Sea People

ACT ONE

SCENE 1 The London Docks with the *Mary Rose* at anchor
SCENE 2 On the Poop Deck of the *Mary Rose*
SCENE 3 The Ship's Galley
SCENE 4 The Poop Deck again
SCENE 5 The Main Deck and the Strange Shipwreck
SCENE 6 Demon Oylslick's Gruesome Grotto
SCENE 7 The *Mary Rose* under the sea

INTERVAL

ACT TWO

SCENE 1 On the shore of the desert island of Tobago
SCENE 2 The Cannibal Village and Stewpot
SCENE 3 At Robinson Crusoe's Stockade
SCENE 4 In the Forest of Grunting Gorillas
SCENE 5 The ruined Temple of the Sacred Snake
SCENE 6 The Voyage Home
SCENE 7 The Nautical Wedding of Robinson Crusoe

The scenery is uncomplicated, Act I being almost a permanent set of the ship whilst Act II is almost a permanent set of the Island.

All the principals can wear one costume throughout, if this is a useful economy, although Crusoe must change to his famous desert island costume and the Dame should change for comedy reasons. The Chorus have just one full change and one minor change.

Please see the scenery notes and production and costume suggestions at the end of the script.

DESCRIPTION OF THE CHARACTERS

Robinson Crusoe is energetic, brave and because he is more intelligent than the rest of the crew (including the Captain) he soon "takes over" in the story. He is continually concerned for his sweetheart, Polly Perkins. He is best played by a female, but can be male.

Polly Perkins, Robinson's girl friend, is attractive but gullible and this causes trouble and danger for our friends in the story.

Captain Perkins is breezy but not too brainy—understandably impatient, and he needs a bit of authority in the drill scene.

Mrs Chrissie Crusoe is a comical pantomime dame but she is sharp and sometimes rescues our friends from danger even if her methods are funny. Male or female.

Bill Barnacle the Bosun and **Ben Dover the Mate**. Bill is a bit stupid but doesn't accept this. Ben is stupid and greatly enjoys the fact. These two parts can be played by extrovert females, or males.

Kenny Crusoe is a cheeky, happy-go-lucky soul and like most of the crew is not very brainy. Usually male, but can be a "second principal boy".

Blackpatch the Pirate comes from Bristol, me dear, so his speech is "Pantomime West Country" and full of "mateys", "me dears", and of course "Jim lad". He is wicked and leering and should play the part with tremendous relish.

Jack Boot is his crony and is just as wicked. If played in a sinister cackling way, it can be played by a female.

Wotta Woppa the Cannibal Queen is tough, devious and has an eye for the men and is funny. She is boisterous and perhaps plump.

Old Jim is an ancient mariner, a small part easily doubled. He can have an "ancient" high-pitched voice and be played by a female.

Lord Nelson has dignity in his short scene and is good-natured when talking to the daft crew. This small part could be played as a second principal boy.

Demon Oylslick is thoroughly nasty and twisted and is played in a slimy, cackling, utterly repulsive way. Male or female.

The Fairy Detergenta is cheerful, confident and triumphant.

Man Friday is a friendly, amiable soul who likes a laugh, and is decidedly extrovert. In most productions of this pantomime he has been played by Jamaicans. Though this idea obviously works well, it is not, of course, essential.

The Chorus They may well be mainly female but with this particular pantomime subject they are extrovert as the ship's crew, even more extrovert as the cannibals and very extrovert indeed as the villainous swaggering pirates.

There have been many professional productions of this script and always the characters of Demon Oylslick and the Fairy Detergenta are taken up by the local press so this fact may be of help with your publicity.

J.M.

Other pantomimes by John Morley from Samuel French

Aladdin
Dick Whittington
Goldilocks and the Three Bears
Jack and the Beanstalk
Sinbad the Sailor

and

Pinocchio
The Wind In The Willows
(based on the story by Kenneth Grahame)

MUSIC SUGGESTIONS

The songs suggested are based on audience research, for pantomime audiences like to hear the songs they know. They like "standards". You are, of course, welcome to alter the choice of songs but please remember that a licence issued by Samuel French Ltd to perform the pantomime does not include permission to use copyright songs and music. Please read the notice supplied by the Performing Right Society, which follows this list of Music Suggestions.

The publishers of the suggested music are given in brackets after the song title.

Overture   Eight bars of *Rule Britannia*. Then a couple of up-tempo songs. Then a triumphant last eights bars of *Rule Britannia* again

ACT I

SONG
1. There's A Tavern In The Town (trad)   **Sailors**
   or
   The Fleet's In (Chappells)
2. We Joined The Navy (Chappells)   **Kenny, Bill** and **Ben**
3. Beyond the Blue Horizon   **Robinson, Captain** and **Sailors**
   or
   In the Navy
   or
   Sailing Along On the Crest of a Wave
4. I Do Like To Be Beside the Seaside (trad)   **Mrs Crusoe** and **Sailors**
5. Fame (I'm Gonna Live Forever) (Music Sales Ltd)   **Robinson** and **Company** (except **Villains**)
6. Presents (to the tune of *Bobby Shafto*—trad)   **Kenny, Robinson, Polly** and **Captain**
7. Spread A Little Happiness (Chappells)   **Robinson** and **Polly**
   or
   Close To You (Music Sales)
   or
   Top Of The World (Music Sales)
8. What Shall We Do With The Drunken Sailor *plus* Sailor's Hornpipe (trad)   **Sailors, Polly** and **Robinson**

9	With Cat-Like Tread (Sullivan, from The Pirates of Penzance)	**Blackpatch, Jack Boot** and **Pirates**
9(a)	I Am A Pirate King (Sullivan, from The Pirates of Penzance)	**Blackpatch** and **Pirates**
10	I'm Forever Blowing Bubbles (E.M.I.) *or* Main theme from *Swan Lake*	**Mrs Crusoe** and **Kenny's Ballet**
11	Spartacus Theme from The Onedin Line—Katchaturian) *or* Fingal's Cave *and* Fame (eight bars reprise)	**The Sea People Dance Routine** **Robinson, Fairy** and **The Sea People**

INTERVAL

ACT II

12	Totem Tom Tom (from *Rose Marie*, Chappells and Samuel French) *or* Civilisation (I Don't Want To Leave The Jungle) (Chappells)	**Wotta Woppa** and **Cannibals**
13	You've Got A Friend (E.M.I.) *or* Friendship (Cole Porter, Chappells) *or* Side By Side (the 1930 song or the Sondheim)	**Robinson** and **Man Friday**
14	California Here I Come (Feldman)	**Man Friday**
15	In The Mood (E.M.I.) *or* I Got Rhythm (Chappells) *or* Hawaiian War Chant (Keith Prowse)	**Cannibals** and **Wotta Woppa**
15(a)	Softly Wakes My Heart (music not lyric, from *Samson and Delilah*, Saint Saens) *or* In A Persian Market Place (Katelby) *or* Kashmiri Song (Pale Hands I Love) (Feldmans)	solo snake dance
16	I Wouldn't Leave My Little Wooden Hut For You (E.M.I.) *or* Jeepers Creepers, Where D'You Get Those Peepers (Feldman)	**Wotta Woppa** and **Blackpatch**

Robinson Crusoe

| 17 | We Are Sailing—songsheet (Music Sales Ltd) Eight bars of *Rule Britannia*, into Finale reprise of Song 4. | **Kenny, Mrs Crusoe** and **Audience All** |

If you have any difficulty obtaining sheet music, FRANCIS MUSIC SUPPLY, 12 GERRARD STREET, LONDON W1, are most helpful.

The following statement concerning the use of music is printed here on behalf of the Performing Right Society Ltd, by whom it was supplied

The permission of the owner of the performing right in copyright music must be obtained before any public performance may be given, whether in conjunction with a play or sketch or otherwise, and this permission is just as necessary for amateur performances as for professional. The majority of copyright musical works (other than oratorios, musical plays and similar dramatico–musical works) are controlled in the British Commonwealth by the PERFORMING RIGHT SOCIETY LTD, 29–33 BERNERS STREET, LONDON W1P 4AA.

The Society's practice is to issue licences authorizing the use of its repertoire to the proprietors of premises at which music is publicly performed, or, alternatively, to the organizers of musical entertainments, but the Society does not require payment of fees by performers as such. Producers or promoters of plays, sketches, etc., at which music is to be performed, during or after the play or sketch, should ascertain whether the premises at which their performances are to be given are covered by a licence issued by the Society, and if they are not, should make application to the Society for particulars as to the fee payable.

COPYRIGHT INFORMATION

(See also page ii)

This play is fully protected under the Copyright Laws of the British Commonwealth of Nations, the United States of America and all countries of the Berne and Universal Copyright Conventions.

All rights, including Stage, Motion Picture, Radio, Television, Public Reading, and Translation into Foreign Languages, are strictly reserved.

No part of this publication may lawfully be reproduced in ANY form or by any means—photocopying, typescript, recording (including video-recording), manuscript, electronic, mechanical, or otherwise—or be transmitted or stored in a retrieval system, without prior permission.

Licences for amateur performances are issued subject to the understanding that it shall be made clear in all advertising matter that the audience will witness an amateur performance; that the names of the authors of the plays shall be included on all announcements and on all programmes; and that the integrity of the authors' work will be preserved.

The Royalty Fee is subject to contract and subject to variation at the sole discretion of Samuel French Ltd.

In Theatres or Halls seating Six Hundred or more the fee will be subject to negotiation.

In Territories Overseas the fee quoted in this Acting Edition may not apply. A fee will be quoted on application to our local authorized agent, or if there is no such agent, on application to Samuel French Ltd, London.

VIDEO RECORDING OF AMATEUR PRODUCTIONS

Please note that the copyright laws governing video-recording are extremely complex and that it should not be assumed that any play may be video-recorded *for whatever purpose* without first obtaining the permission of the appropriate agents. The fact that a play is published by Samuel French Ltd does not indicate that video rights are available or that Samuel French Ltd controls such rights.

PROLOGUE

After the Overture, to set up the style of the pantomime, a voice is heard through the front of house speakers—or the Captain enters through the front curtains—declaiming the Prologue as though telling a pirate adventure story

Prologue A long time ago, down by the docks in London Town, someone possessed a fabulous treasure chart. This is the story of the treasure—the story of the desert island where it lay hidden—the story of the sailor who found it. His name?

There is a quick fanfare

ROBINSON CRUSOE! So come to where the adventure begins—come to the docks of London Town!

Music is heard, the Curtains open

ACT I

Scene 1

The London docks, with the "Mary Rose" at anchor (see Scenery notes)

Captain Perkins, Polly, the Sailors (and perhaps their girls) are singing and dancing

Song 1 and OPENING ROUTINE

Soon a group embark on a square dance while the others clap in time, wolf whistle and shout "That's it, Bill", "Shake a leg, Jenny", etc

After the routine the Dancers and Chorus drift off, variously

Polly and the Captain are left alone

Captain (*pointing to the ship*) Well, Polly, it'll soon be time for me to sail on the *Mary Rose*.
Polly (*excitedly*) Oh yes, Father. Mrs Crusoe and I have started to get things ready in the galley!
Captain (*angrily*) I'm the Captain and I've told you twenty times. You and Mrs Crusoe *are not going*.
Polly But we've been on every other voyage—what's so different about this one?
Captain We're sailing to the West Indies and they're famous for—
Polly They're famous for rum and sugar and that's what you're going to bring back to London!

Captain No daughter. They're famous for *pirates*.

There is a dramatic chord

Polly (*laughing*) Pirates! Just a stupid story!
Captain Do you want to be cut to pieces by a pirate cutlass?
Polly Oh, Father! (*Deliberately changing the subject*) I wonder where everyone is? Buying last minute things for the voyage I expect! (*She laughs*) I wonder what Kenny Crusoe is buying?
Captain (*looking off*) Here he is now—we'll soon find out.

Vaudeville music is heard and Kenny enters with a yellow parrot in a cage

Kenny (*to the Audience*) Hullo—I'm Kenny Crusoe! Yes, my name is Kenny C. Crusoe!
Polly What's the C for?
Kenny For ships to sail on—what d'you think the sea's for? Are you looking forward to the voyage, Polly?
Captain I'm not letting Mrs Crusoe and my daughter go on this voyage and *that is final*.

The Captain strides to the wings followed by the protesting Polly

Polly Father, be reasonable! You know we can help you! Father!

The Captain and Polly exit. Kenny shrugs, mystified

Kenny (*to the Audience*) I've been buying things for the voyage and all good sailors take a parrot, don't they? (*He holds up the cage*) Like the parrot? Ten pound fifty at Tesco's—oh, I've forgotten to feed him! (*He runs to the wings and collects a huge prop packet marked* POLLYFILLA. *He holds it up and tips the corner as though putting food in the cage*) I've just bought him. Well, the man in the shop said it was going cheap so I said yes, I can hear it is. Well, budgies always go cheep don't they? (*Showing the Audience the cage*) He's nice, isn't he?
Audience YES!
Kenny Well I'm going to keep him for *myself*. I found him on a telegraph wire telephoning—d'you know what he's called?
Audience Busby!
Kenny (*laughing*) Ooooo, you are quick! He wants to come on the journey 'cos he thinks we're going to the Canary Islands! And he's very easy to look after. All he likes to eat is Shredded Tweet, Bird's Custard and then for afters this Pollyfilla. Now I know some sailor will try and pinch him, so will you look after him for me?
Audience Yes!
Kenny I was only born with two ears, so I'm a bit deaf. I can't hear you. *Will you look after him for me?*
Audience YES!
Kenny I know what I'll do. (*He crosses to* DR *corner*) I'll hang him up over here, out of harm's way. (*He puts the cage on a hook*) If anyone tries to nick my bird, will you shout "Busby"? (*He moves* CS)
Audience YES!

Act I, Scene 1   3

Kenny We'll have a test. I'll pretend I'm someone else, not me. (*He stalks over to the cage*)
Audience Busby!
Kenny BEAUTIFUL! Mind you, I don't think anyone knows he's there. I don't think I need to bother with all this warning business, I mean, if I thought someone else would try and nick him I'd . . .

Someone enters and tries to steal Busby

Audience BUSBY!
Kenny Getartoffit!

Kenny chases the person off

Thanks for looking after him. See you soon! Bye!

Kenny exits, waving

The Lights dim, leaving a green spot DL

Blackpatch the Pirate enters to dramatic music

Blackpatch (*with a Bristol accent*) Arrrrrrr! Good mornin' to 'eeeee, mateys! Well let's get one thing clear from the start. I'm Blackpatch the Pirate and you are a load of (*local name*) Wishwash! (*With a threatening roar*) Don't yer answer me back mateys or I'll come down there with me blunderbuss and blow yer brains out! (*He fires his pistol. It either has a "cracker tape" in it or a gun is fired from offstage — either way, the effect is an anti-climax after his threat. Looking at the gun*) I was hoping for more noise than that, me dears. I've just bought it down at (*local store*) and I've been swindled. (*He points to someone in the front row of the Audience*) Arr, Jim lad, I've been swindled and them as swindles Captain Blackpatch lives to regret it. (*To all the Audience*) Now mateys, a pirate needs three things: a blunderbuss, a cutlass and a parrot. (*Seeing the cage*) Well, polish me poop deck, there *is* a parrot!

As Blackpatch goes to the cage the Audience shouts "Busby"

Kenny runs on

Kenny Thanks, kids! (*To Blackpatch*) What d'you think you're doing, pinching my parrot? You stupid great ignorant oaf, you clumsy clodhopper with—
Blackpatch (*roaring*) OOaarrrargh!
Kenny (*terrified*) I'm sorry, sir, didn't mean it, sir, sorry, sorry.
Blackpatch You can help me, matey. (*Pointing to the ship*) Is that there ship about to sail?
Kenny (*in a very high voice*) Yes, matey. (*Clearing his throat and speaking with a very deep voice*) Yes, matey.
Blackpatch Is it by any chance going to the West Indies?

Kenny nods frantically

And is it by any chance going to far off Jamaiccy?

Kenny nods in terror again

That's two thousand nautical miles—(*condescendingly*)—knots to you.
Kenny Knots to you, too.
Blackpatch That means I must think of a way to start a mutiny on board. (*Pleased with the idea*) A mutiny! Tell me what you know about the Mutiny on the Bounty?
Kenny What?
Blackpatch Tell me about the Bounty!
Kenny Well it's made of toffee and coconut and it's covered in milk chocolate and—
Blackpatch I'll cover you in milk chocolate if you start being bumptious with me. And one last thing, matey, before you go. If you tells one soul that you've met me I'll (*prodding Kenny in the chest at each word*) have—your—guts—for—garters.
Kenny (*prodding Blackpatch back*) I—won't—tell—a—soul.
Blackpatch (*growling*) OOaarrrargh!
Kenny (*retreating*) Yes, well, goodbye, nice meeting you, so long—oh—oh—oeuurr!

Kenny's retreats have got faster and faster and he now runs offstage in a panic

Blackpatch (*confidentially to the Audience*) I'll tell 'eee why I wants to know if that ship is bound for Jamaiccy. Near Jamaiccy lies a secret treasure! I've heard on the pirate grapevine that someone who's here in the London Docks is the sailor wot's got the treasure *chart*. BUT WHO IS HE, MATEYS? I must get that chart! Then I'll soon get the treasure because I'm not only a pirate . . . (*He takes a book from his waistband*) I also dabbles in black magic and this 'ere book is my magic book. You don't believe me, but listen 'ere, mateys. (*He opens the book and reads out the spell*)

"Abracadabra abracadee
Signs of the Zodiac one, two, three
Spirits of evil harken to me!"

Strange music begins and a spotlight comes up on a barrel by the upstage wings. A hideous black creeper starts to grow up several feet (nylon line)

Look, mateys, deadly nightshade! Me favourite flower! (*He points to the creeper and calls out*)

Spirits of evil that we fear
Now make the flower disappear!

Strange music is heard again and the (weighted) creeper sinks down into the barrel

But I must away—I must depart!
'Cos I *must* find that there treasure chart!
Ha ha ha ha!

Blackpatch exits to "boos" from the Audience

Loud vaudeville music—or the "Sailor's Hornpipe"—heralds the entrance of Bill the Bosun and Ben the Mate

Act I, Scene 1

They are holding a cut-out of a small boat or canoe with "Blue Peter" written across its bow. The boat is only two feet deep so we can clearly see their legs as they march across the stage

Bill (*shouting*) Ship ahoy!
Ben (*shouting*) Come in number nine! Come in number nine! Your time's up!

Ben pushes the boat into the far wings while Bill addresses the audience

Bill (*with a naval salute*) I'm Barnacle Bill the Bosun!
Ben (*with a comedy salute, arm going round like a windmill*) And I'm Ben Dover the Mate! (*To the Audience, laughing*) Ben Dover! Isn't it a ridiculous name!
Bill (*importantly*) Yes, we're part of the crew of that ship over there. We're Bill and Ben—
Ben (*proudly*) The Flower Pot Men.
Bill (*sarcastically*) Why would a couple of sailors like us be Flower Pot Men?
Ben (*proudly*) Because we're potty!
Bill (*hitting Ben*) Will you shut up!
Ben Don't you hit me like that when I'm talking to my friends. (*To the Audience*) Well, folks, it's fabulous meeting you all like this. It's really nice and I just want to say—
Bill (*shouting at Ben*) Shut yer bilgepipe!
Ben I'm only—
Bill Batten yer hatches!
Ben But I haven't—
Bill Pull yourself together. If you don't watch it Captain Perkins won't take you on as Mate because as a sailor you are *useless!*
Ben I'm not, I'm not, I'm *not!* (*He stamps his foot*)
Bill All right then, tell me about the ship over there. Go on, tell me about the bulwarks, the starboard and the port side.
Ben Port side? We're going to Egypt then?
Bill No we're *not* going to Egypt. Port side is on the *left!* Now tell me where the bulwarks are.
Ben The bulwarks?
Bill Yes, the bulwarks.
Ben Well, starboard is on the right, port side is on the left and in the middle there's a funny little hut for the cow.
Bill "A funny little hut for the cow"? What are you talking about—"A funny little hut for the cow".
Ben That's where the bull walks! Ha, ha, ha!
Bill Where the bull— (*Reluctantly he explodes with laughter as well*) Ha, ha, ha!

Kenny enters as Bill and Ben are laughing

Kenny I'm surprised to see you two laughing—I thought you didn't want to go on this voyage?
Bill }
Ben } (*together*) We don't.
Kenny Then why did you join up?

Bill \
Ben } (*together*) Same reason as you!

They sing, and soon Kenny joins them, for

Song 2

The song includes a short dance

Kenny exits after the song

Ben happily sings a section of the song, unaccompanied. Then there is dramatic music and the Lights darken

Blackpatch enters, a green spot picking him up

Ben, looking at his feet, bumps into Blackpatch, and stops laughing. He puts out his hands and feels his way upwards, then sees Blackpatch's face

Ben (*with a little scream*) Aaaah! It's Sweeney Todd! \
Bill (*scared*) It's Blackpatch the Pirate! \
Ben (*looking at Blackpatch in the green spotlight*) Is it? It looks like the Jolly Green Giant! \
Blackpatch (*insulted and angry*) I am Blackpatch. \
Ben Very pleased to meet you, Mr Backscratch. \
Blackpatch (*roaring at him*) Blackpatch! Blackpatch! \
Both All fall down! \
Bill I'm Bill Barnacle, the Bosun and I'm looking for work. \
Ben I'm Ben Dover, the Mate and I'm looking for a way to get out of here fast. (*He starts to move away*) \
Bill (*pointing at Ben; sternly*) SITTT.

Ben sits like a dog and looks up at Bill with tongue out, panting loudly

And now— \
Ben Walkies! \
Blackpatch Come 'ere.

Bill and Ben do not move

Come 'ere!

Bill and Ben take one big step towards Blackpatch

I want some information from you two drop-outs. \
Bill \
Ben } (*together*) No!

Blackpatch draws his pistol and threatens them

Bill \
Ben } (*together*) Yes! \
Blackpatch That boat over there—is she going to Jamaiccy? \
Bill Yes! \
Blackpatch Is she going to a desert island called . . . Tobago? \
Ben Lovely. Pour a bit of tinned fruit on it and it's smashing.

Act I, Scene 1

Blackpatch *Tobago.*
Ben I thought you said Sago! (*To the Audience*) I did! I thought he said ...
Blackpatch One more word out of you and I'll blow off yer right ear lobe. I've got quite a collection of right ear lobes that belongs to sailors as is cheeky to Cap'n Blackpatch.
Ben (*to the Audience*) Kinky!
Bill What do you wish us to do, oh powerful one? Oh great and important pirate, oh king of the seven seas?
Ben (*aside to Bill*) Creep!
Blackpatch You two are going to help me. You are going to do a dirty deed.
Ben I'm not doing a dirty deed. (*To the Audience*) Dirty deeds are naughty, aren't they?
Bill Oh no, they're not.
Ben (*with the Audience*) Oh yes, they are.
Blackpatch (*to the Audience*) Silence! If you don't keep silent you won't hear the plot! (*To the two sailors*) I'm going to stow aboard Robinson Crusoe's ship and when we reach Tobago, I'm hoping to meet up with *another* ship—a pirate one!
Bill But where does the dirty deed come in?
Blackpatch You two are going to help me—you're going to become pirates.
Ben (*frightened*) Me become a pirate?
Bill It's easy. You just take the oath.
Ben Where shall I take it?
Bill You don't take it anywhere.
Blackpatch You take the oath and you take it quick. Understand?
Ben (*nodding*) You mean, Quick Quaker Oats?
Bill (*hitting Ben*) Not oats, oathththth.
Ben Stop splashing me. (*He wipes his face*)
Blackpatch Take the oath. Repeat after me. (*Holding up his hand*) "I swear"—
Ben (*shocked*) I'm not going to swear!
Blackpatch (*sternly*) "I swear"—
Ben Damn.
Bill No, you've got to swear properly, like a proper pirate. Put your hand up and say the wicked word.
Ben (*with his hand up*) Gym slips!

The "Pirate Swearing In" is called out quickly

Blackpatch Repeat after me. I hereby swear—
Bill I hereby swear—
Ben I hereby swear—
Blackpatch That I will do dirty deeds—
Bill That I will do dirty deeds—
Ben That I will have dirty knees—
Blackpatch And laugh at officialdom often—
Bill And laugh at officialdom often—
Ben And the Wombles of Wimbledon Common—
Blackpatch To the best of my limited ability—

Bill To the best of my limited ability—
Ben To the best of my filletted debility—
Blackpatch To be a crying disgrace and no good to anybody—
Bill To be a crying disgrace and no good to anybody—
Ben To be a frying shoelace and Little Noddy—
Blackpatch So long live lucrative piracy! (*Spitting on his hand*)
Bill So long live lucrative piracy—(*spitting on his hand*)
Ben So long live Lulu and Chuck Berry!
Blackpatch And now . . . cut your throat.
Ben Thank you, and good night.
Blackpatch (*pleased*) Aaaarrr! Ha-harrrrr! Now you're a sworn pirate so what am I going to give 'eee?
Ben A bar of old Jamaiccy!
Blackpatch Now you is sworn in, I'll take you for a drink—come on. You understand your instructions?

Bill nods his head and recites

Bill   When we are sailing out to sea
                And spot the pirate boat
Blackpatch   You're going to be a great help to me
                If you're not—I'll cut yer throat!

Bill and Ben react with comedy terror

   Ooooooooo—hahaha! Yo—ho!

Blackpatch exits

Bill Ooooooo—hahaha! Yo—ho!

Bill exits

Ben (*in a squeaky voice*) Ooooo—hahaha! (*He bursts into tears*) Boo—hoo—hoooo.

Ben has attempted a pirate laugh like the other two but exits, crying, instead

The Captain and Sailors enter elsewhere and gather at the quayside

1st Sailor Where's the Captain? I haven't signed on yet!
Captain I'm here.
2nd Sailor (*looking around*) Where's the signing-on form?
Captain I've put it in my pocket—or did I give it to my daughter—perhaps it's over here . . .

The Captain searches desperately for papers

3rd Sailor Where's the pen?
Captain Er . . .
1st Sailor (*fed up*) The only person who can organize this is Robinson Crusoe.
1st Chorus But where *is* Robinson Crusoe?
2nd Chorus Why don't we give him a call? (*Shouting off*) Robinson!
All Crusoe! It's Robinson! Hullo, Crusoe!

Act I, Scene 1

Robinson Crusoe enters from the ship and waves, then strides forward and shakes hands with the crew

Robinson Hullo! Hullo, Bill! Nice to see you again, Paddy! Morning, Joe—you coming on the voyage?
Joe Aye, Robinson.
Robinson You look well, Harry.
Harry Thanks, Robinson.
Robinson And Captain Perkins! (*He salutes the Captain*) But what's wrong, Captain?
Captain I've lost the signing-on forms.
Robinson They're in your pocket—and the pen's on the floor!

Robinson points and all the others laugh

I hope that's all that's worrying you?
Captain No it's not, Robinson. I'm worried about the pirates we keep hearing about.
Robinson (*to everyone*) Oh, we needn't worry about them, need we?
All No!
Robinson We're all prepared aren't we?
All Yes!
Robinson 'Cos here's a secret weapon! (*He holds up a big catapult from his belt*) There!
Captain But that's just a catapult!
Robinson Maybe it is, but watch! One! (*He aims at a pub sign hanging on the scenery—no need for anything in the catapult sling. He "fires", we hear percussion effect and the pub sign falls to the floor*) Two! (*He aims at some crates piled up at the upstage wings. A swanee whistle is heard and the top crate is whisked off on a wire*) Three! (*He aims at a sailor wearing a hat—percussion effect and the hat whizzes off on a wire*)
    Oh, I can hit every pirate in sight
    Yes, I'm all set for the voyage all right!

Robinson, the Captain and the Sailors sing:

Song 3

PRODUCTION ROUTINE

Robinson (*to the Audience, after the routine*) I must go and tell my Mum that we'll be sailing soon. My Mum loves ships—she spends hours and hours on the boating pool at (*local place*). Come on—let's go and find her! (*Calling*) Mum! Where are you, Mum!
All Mrs Crusoe! Where's Mrs Crusoe!

Everyone exits downstage

As they exit Mrs Crusoe enters upstage to the bouncy theme of Song 3, carrying a brightly coloured plastic bucket like a handbag. She is wearing a Wren's uniform

Mrs Crusoe Hello everybody! Yes, it's me—Chrissie Crusoe! I'm Robinson's

Mum! My other son is Kenny Crusoe and we're all going off on the boat for a lovely trip! (*She walks along the front stage area and trips*) Oooops—that was a lovely trip as well! (*Explaining merrily*) Trip—lovely trip—then *I* tripped—ha, ha, ha! (*She laughs then sees the Audience isn't with her at all*) Forget it. Yes, we're all going off on a boat across the Pedantic Ocean. Yes, we're going to the West Undies. I'm not sure if I've got the name of the place right—I might have made a bloomer there. Well I'm the ship's cook and I'm a very *good* cook. The Captain said he likes my plum duff so much he's going to bring it up at the next meeting with the crew. I've just been shopping in case we run into a storm at sea. Yes, I've bought a mackintosh. As a matter of fact I've bought a *pound* of mackintoshes—anyone like one? Would you? They're Devonshire Creams—(*to someone in the Audience*) They're quite safe dear—suck it and see—here. (*She throws a toffee to the person*) Well, take the paper off before you eat it, you greedy thing! (*She throws out toffees in various directions*) Yes I think I'm going to be the ship's cook again on this voyage so I've been to the Butchers as well! I said, "Have you got anything nice to show me?" and he said "Well I can show you my kidneys", so I said "I'm not interested in your kidneys, I want you to show me a nice joint"—so he showed me this! (*She holds up a scraggy piece of meat*) I looked at it and I said "How much?" and he said "Eight pound fifty." (*Indignantly*) Eight pound fifty for this! I think it would have been cheaper to have seen his kidneys! Then he said "Would you prefer a bird?" and he gave me *this!* (*She holds up a chicken*) He said "It's a pullet." I said "Pullet? I think I'll have to stuff it!" (*She "switches on" the chicken and two small bulbs light up*) Oh look, it's a battery hen! (*She laughs*) Oh dear, life's all go isn't it? And I love being a ship's cook and going on a voyage! Mind you, *after* a voyage I do like coming back home to the seaside. Oh I *love* the seaside—well it's so friendly isn't it? (*She begins to sing boisterously*)

Song 4

Mrs Crusoe sings the first four lines of the song, then stops. Probably a few of the Audience will have started to join in the "tiddley-om-pom-pom" but she pretends that they haven't

(*To the Audience, utterly disgusted with them*) Silence. Not a sound. Not a flipping word from one of you. (*Exasperated*) Look, I'm Mrs Crusoe and I'm singing about the seaside and that bit where you forgot to join in is a *famous* bit! When I say "Where the brass band plays," *you* have to *be* the brass band and say "Tiddley—om—pom—pom!" Let's have another try! (*She calls out*) "When the brass band plays—"

She conducts as the Audience feebly replies "Tiddley-om-pom-pom"

What? I can't hear a thing! Once again! (*She shouts out loudly*) "Where the brass band plays—"
Audience Tiddley-om-pom-pom!
Mrs Crusoe Beautiful! Lovely noise! You're not the brass band, you're the Liverpool Philharmonic! Fabulous!

Act I, Scene 1   11

Mrs Crusoe sings and claps her hands, encouraging the Audience to join in the clapping and the chorus line

   Fantastic! (*She beckons off*) Come on, darlings! I'm telling them we all love the seaside—and we do, don't we?

   The Sailors (and perhaps their girls) enter

   Sailors (*variously*) Yes, we like the sea, all right. Hullo, Mrs Crusoe. Well, if it isn't Chrissie!
   Mrs Crusoe (*to the Audience*) Once again and clap in time—come on! That's it! Clap!

   Mrs Crusoe, the Sailors and the Audience sing and clap and she calls out "Fabulous!" after the "Tiddley-om-pom-pom"

SHORT PRODUCTION NUMBER

Mrs Crusoe marches to and fro along the footlights while the Sailors sing and dance

After the song, all exit, Mrs Crusoe waving and calling out "See you later!"

Polly enters, calling, followed by the Captain

Polly Mrs Crusoe! Mrs Crusoe!

   Mrs Crusoe returns

Mrs Crusoe What is it, dear?
Polly Father won't let us go on the voyage—he says it's too dangerous.
Mrs Crusoe What? I'll see about that. (*She walks up aggressively to the Captain*) Now look here, Captain Onedin—
Captain How dare you!
Mrs Crusoe All right then, Captain Birdseye—
Captain (*emphatically, loudly, waving his fists*) No women on board! No women on board!
Mrs Crusoe (*imitating him with a squeaky voice and similar fist waving*) "No women on board! No women on board!"
Captain Definitely no! The West Indies are infested with pirates and those men are real brutes.
Mrs Crusoe (*thrilled*) Oh, how lovely!
Captain Who is it spend their lives throwing daggers, fighting duels and firing pistols?
Mrs Crusoe Manchester United supporters.
Captain No. Some great big nasty creature will steal your money.
Mrs Crusoe You mean . . . (*the present Chancellor*)
Captain I mean pirates. You two are not sailing and that's final.
Polly (*whispering to Mrs Crusoe*) What'll we do?
Mrs Crusoe (*whispering back*) I'll get us aboard that ship if it kills me. Chrissie Crusoe never admits defeat. We'll think of something . . .

   She exits with Polly, explaining some apparently very complicated plan to her

Captain (*to the Audience*) Women!

The Captain exits the other side

Old Jim enters, hobbling on a crutch, with Robinson

Old Jim Robinson!
Robinson It's Old Jim! Why weren't you signing on?
Old Jim Seafaring is finished for this old seadog.
Robinson But I'll look after you like I always do!
Old Jim Aye, you've always been very kind to me, you 'as.
Robinson Nonsense!
Old Jim And becos of that kindness, see, I've got a little something for 'ee, Robinson . . .

Mysterious music starts. The Lights fade down to just a spot on the two of them as Old Jim fumbles in his shirt front

Robinson I don't want anything from you, you're my friend!
Old Jim Aye, and friend must help a friend. (*He pulls out a crumpled piece of canvas about two feet square. There is a dramatic chord*)
Robinson (*wondrously*) The Treasure Chart of Tobago!!! Great Scott—so you're it's owner!
Old Jim And shiver me timbers, there's no-one in the world as deserved it more than 'eeeee.
Robinson (*emotionally*) Jim . . . if I find the treasure I'll give you half, I promise . . .
Old Jim I won't be 'ere, matey. I'll be dead and gorn. Read it to me so I can hear them secret words for the last time . . .
Robinson (*reading*) "Captain Kidd's Treasure"

There is a dramatic chord and upstage (unseen by Old Jim and Robinson) Blackpatch enters. He reacts hugely to what he hears

Robinson "The treasure lies within a mile
Near palm trees on a desert isle."
Blackpatch (*with a loud ecstatic whisper*) At last—the treasure chart!
Robinson And there's a cannibal village . . .

Old Jim nods, as Robinson points to the chart

Then the jungle . . .

Old Jim nods, as he and Robinson study the chart

Blackpatch But how can I steal it? I know, I'll stow away on board and bide me time! (*Triumphantly*) Robinson Crusoe's not the only one bound for Jamaiccy! Ha! ha! ha! (*Reciting*)
I'm horrible, hideous, moody and mean
So I'll climb aboard—I've not been seen!

Blackpatch exits into the ship

Robinson (*emotionally, shaking Old Jim's hand*) I'll never forget you, Jim, never.

Act I, Scene 1

Old Jim God bless 'ee, shipmate, and may the Northern Star watch over 'ee . . .

Old Jim hobbles off

Robinson The chart . . . I can't believe it . . . *we're going to be rich!* I must call everybody! (*He calls out left and right*) Everybody—look—it's the Treasure Chart of Tobago! Gold, silver, diamonds! (*In his excitement he strides down to the corner where Busby is*)
Audience Busby!

Kenny runs in

Kenny Thanks, kids!

Mrs Crusoe, Bill, Ben, the Captain, Polly and the Sailors enter excitedly

Robinson Captain Perkins, will you let us all stop off at Tobago—because that's where the treasure is!
Captain Well . . . it's *en route* to Jamaica but I don't know . . .
Mrs Crusoe ⎫   Oh, Captain dear!
Bill and Ben ⎬ (*together*) It's the treasure!
Kenny   ⎬   We'll be rich!
Polly   ⎭   Father!
Sailors (*threateningly*) Captain Perkins!
Captain (*smiling*) All right!
All Hooray!
Polly (*sadly; to Robinson*) Then goodbye Robinson, darling.

Polly and Robinson hold hands tenderly

Robinson Goodbye, Polly. Don't worry about me . . .
Polly (*acting out grief*) Oh . . .
Mrs Crusoe (*sadly; to the Captain*) Then goodbye Captain, darling.

Mrs Crusoe and Captain hold hands in the same tender way

Captain Goodbye, Chrissie. Don't worry about me . . .
Mrs Crusoe (*acting out grief*) Oh . . . come, Polly . . .

Mrs Crusoe and Polly exit together, with a pretence at grief

Music for Song 5 starts

Robinson (*speaking over the music and waving the chart*) To the Island of Treasure! To the Island of Tobago!

Robinson begins to sing and the others join in with him

Song 5 (or a reprise of Song 3)
SHORT PRODUCTION NUMBER

Whilst all are engaged in the Production Number Mrs Crusoe and Polly enter with two large cardboard boxes which completely cover them apart from their legs and feet. The "boxes" attempt to cross the stage during the routine and after some bumps manage to get to the gang plank and exit on to the ship

As the song draws to a close everyone exits on to the ship, the last to leave being Robinson who waves to the Audience as he goes

Black-out

Scene 2

On the Poop Deck (tabs or frontcloth—see scenery notes)

There is sinister music playing and the lighting is dim. Blackpatch enters holding a telescope

Blackpatch So, Robinson Crusoe and his friends are all aboard—but there's *someone else* aboard isn't there, mateys? Someone whose name makes people tremble from Pirbright to Persia, from Surbiton to Singapore, from Kingston to Karachi—*me!* (*Note. Please make these place names local by choosing three and then add them to the alliterate words, such as "From Manchester to Mexico" or "From Bearwood to Bombay", etc*) Yes, here we are on the high seas, on the way to the island of treasure—a treasure that will be mine! (*He looks off and starts*) A ship on the horizon! (*He puts the telescope to his eye*) Well, button me britches, that's a skull and cross-bones flying from the mast! (*Putting the telescope down*) A pirate ship! When it's nearer I'll signal it! (*Reciting*)
    When you're evil and crooked and ruthless like me
    You're always the winner—just you wait and see!
    Ha ha ha ha ha ha!

Blackpatch exits

A few bars of comedy/spooky music are played and Mrs Crusoe and Polly creep across the stage, closely followed by the Captain

Mrs Crusoe (*pleased*) We stowed away and we still haven't been found!
Polly No-one knows we're here!
Captain (*sternly*) I do!

Mrs Crusoe and Polly freeze

Polly I can hear someone!
Mrs Crusoe Sounds like Ken Livingstone!

Mrs Crusoe and Polly both turn round

Captain (*furiously*) You stupid, empty-headed, irresponsible, crackpotted woman!
Mrs Crusoe Don't you dare call me a woman!
Captain My *own daughter.*
Polly I'm sorry, Father. We stowed away so that we could help you!
Mrs Crusoe Yes we—
Captain (*still furious*) Do you know the penalty? Have you any idea what the penalty is?

Act I, Scene 2   15

Mrs Crusoe Of course I have. If you kick the ball when you're offside...
Captain Silence! (*Pointing to Mrs Crusoe*) The penalty for stowing away is laid down in ship's orders. It's twenty pounds.
Mrs Crusoe (*wailing*) Twenty pounds? But I can't pay that!
Captain Polly, go to your cabin. I want to sort this out with Mrs Crusoe.
Polly (*distressed*) I'm so sorry, Mrs Crusoe. Perhaps you can borrow some money from someone?

Polly exits

Mrs Crusoe (*to the Audience*) What a nice girl Polly is. But I couldn't have the cheek to borrow twenty quid from anybody. I wouldn't have the nerve! It would be awful! (*To the Captain*) Can I borrow twenty quid?
Captain Certainly not.
Mrs Crusoe You're so stern the way you say that. So stern—and so *masterly*.
Captain (*flattered*) Masterly?
Mrs Crusoe Yes. Like Captain Hook. He discovered Ambrosia.
Captain You mean Captain Cook who discovered Australia.
Mrs Crusoe Yes. Like him as well. He was masterly... (*with cunning*)... and he was generous. Always lending people money, he was. Smashing feller. Everyone liked him. Well he was *generous* you see. And if you're generous, people do like you. (*She looks at the Captain; in a sudden, deep, sultry voice*) Oh my word, you're so attractive and fascinating. Turn your face sideways. You've got a nose like Basil Brush.
Captain Oh, Chrissie, I was wondering if you felt like that about me. (*Flirting heavily*) You're a little devil—you drive me mad!
Mrs Crusoe (*to the Audience*) He fancies me! That means if I play my cards right, he'll lend me the twenty quid! Just watch this. (*To the Captain*) I know the crew call you Captain Perkins but I've got another name for you.
Captain What's that?
Mrs Crusoe Burt Reynolds.
Captain (*huskily*) Chrissie. (*He takes some pound notes from his pocket*) Oh, Chrissie Crusoe...

The Captain holds the money by his side. Mrs Crusoe reaches out and takes the notes from him, gazing into his eyes

Mrs Crusoe Burt. (*She snatches the money from him*)
Captain (*realizing*) I've lent you the money!
Mrs Crusoe Now don't be curt, Burt. I'm hurt when you flirt and then you're curt. One minute it's a cert, and next minute I'm just a pert bit of skirt flung in the dirt.
Captain I'm sorry, Chrissie. It's just that I don't like lending money like this.
Mrs Crusoe Why not?
Captain Well, what proof have I got that you'll ever pay me back?
Mrs Crusoe I'll write out an I.O.U.
Captain What's an I.O.U?
Mrs Crusoe (*to the Audience*) Now you see why my son, Robinson, is really in charge of this ship. (*Nodding towards the Captain*) He may be the Captain but he's a bit thick, isn't he? (*To the Captain*) An I.O.U. is a piece

of paper that states quite clearly that one person owes the other person some money.

Captain I'm so dizzy at the very thought of you, I can't concentrate on what you're saying.

Mrs Crusoe (*explaining*) I've got to make out an I.O.U. (*Taking some paper from her bosom*) Now I've got a bit of paper, so can I borrow a pencil?

Captain Certainly. (*He gives her a pencil from his pocket*)

Mrs Crusoe Now ... (*Writing*) "I.O.U. twenty pounds." There.

Captain (*proudly*) And that's my I.O.U., isn't it?

Mrs Crusoe Yes, that's your I.O.U. And as it's your I.O.U., you, of course, have to sign it.

Captain Of course. (*He takes the pencil and paper, signs his signature with a flourish then gives the pencil back to Mrs Crusoe*)

Mrs Crusoe There we are! That was simple wasn't it! Good-day! (*She starts to exit*)

Captain (*realization dawning*) Hey! Just a minute! You must think me a mug!

Mrs Crusoe (*innocently*) I think you a mug? Why should I think you a mug? (*Anxiously, to the Audience*) He's got me, I've had it now.

Captain Why should you think me a mug? (*Loudly and indignantly*) Because you've still got my pencil!

Mrs Crusoe laughs

My pencil! I want my pencil!

The Captain chases Mrs Crusoe off, to a few bars of vaudeville music

The other side Polly enters with a plastic carrier bag

Polly (*looking round and calling*) Father! Where has Father got to ... (*Her search takes her close to Busby's cage*)

Audience Busby!

Kenny runs on holding two carrier bags

Kenny (*to the Audience*) Thanks, kids!

Robinson enters holding a bag

Polly
Kenny } (*together*) Father! Captain! Captain Perkins!
Robinson

Captain Perkins enters with a carrier bag

Robinson (*to the Captain*) We don't need the stuff in these bags so shall we throw it overboard? (*He is about to throw his carrier bag into the wings or the band area*)

Kenny Stop, Robinson! (*To the Audience*) You'd like the stuff wouldn't you?

Audience Yes!

Kenny I thought you might!

Captain (*shocked*) You mean give the stuff away as though it was *presents*?

Polly
Kenny } (*together*) That's right. *Presents!*
Robinson

Act I, Scene 2   17

They all form a line—Robinson, Captain, Polly and lastly Kenny, and they sing at a fast pace

                      Song 6: Presents

                      (To the tune of "Bobby Shafto")

All Four   We have got some presents here
                       We have got some presents here
                       We have got some presents here
                       That we'd like to give to you!

Kenny steps forward and attempts to sing

Kenny   I have got some—

But Robinson sings instead, and Kenny retires muttering and complaining bitterly

Robinson   I have got some sweeties here
                       I have got some sweeties here
                       I have got some sweeties here
                       That I'd like to give to you!

During the instrumental vamp music Robinson collects sweets from his bag

    (Calling) Who wants some sweets? You? All right—here goes. *(He throws sweets to the Audience)* And you? All right then!

Robinson throws a couple more, then all four continue singing

All Four   We have got some presents here
                       We have got some presents here
                       We have got some presents here
                       That we'd like to give you!

Kenny again steps forward to sing

Kenny   I have got some—

But the Captain has stepped forward instead, so again Kenny retires muttering and complaining bitterly, while the Captain sings

Captain   I have got some comics here
                       I have got some comics here
                       I have got some comics here
                       That I'd like to give you!

And, over the linking vamp music the Captain calls out as he collects the items from his carrier bag

    (Calling) Who wants a comic? Here's Action Man! You want Beano? All right! *(He throws them)*

All Four   We have got some presents here
                       We have got some presents here
                       We have got some presents here
                       That we'd like to give to you!

Kenny again steps forward to sing
Kenny　　　　　　I have got some—
But Polly steps forward instead so Kenny retires muttering furiously to himself
Polly　　　　　　I have got some pencils here
　　　　　　　　　　I have got some pencils here
　　　　　　　　　　I have got some pencils here
　　　　　　　　　　That I'd like to give you!
And over the linking vamp music Polly collects pencils from her carrier bag
　　　　(*Calling*) Who wants a pencil? You do? Okay—catch this! (*She throws a pencil*) Hands up who wants a pencil! You—here you are!
All Four　　　　We have got some presents here
　　　　　　　　　　We have got some presents here
　　　　　　　　　　We have got some presents here
　　　　　　　　　　That we'd like to give you!
Kenny again steps forward

Kenny (*calling out*) Stop everything! This is the moment you've all been waiting for! My turn now. Well you've had sweeties and comics and pencils but, oh boy, get ready for this! Oh yum yum! Delicious, Fabulous!
　(*Singing*)　　　　I have got some fresh eggs here
　　　　　　　　　　I have got some fresh eggs here
　　　　　　　　　　I have got some fresh eggs here
　　　　　　　　　　That I'd like to give you!

Kenny takes from his carrier a cardboard crate of eggs. He opens it and holds up an egg

(*To the Audience*) Shall I?
Polly　⎫
Robinson　⎬ (*together*) No! (*The Audience will join in with the "No"*)
Captain　⎭
Kenny (*to the Audience*) Shall I?
Polly　⎫
Robinson　⎬ (*together*) No, Kenny! Give them a chance!
Captain　⎭
Kenny (*to the Audience*) No? All right then—I will!

Percussion is heard as Kenny prepares to throw out an egg—in fact a table tennis ball—whilst the other three watch anxiously

Polly　　　　⎫
Robinson　⎬ (*together*　Don't Kenny! He's going to throw it! Watch out all
Captain　　⎭ *severally*)　of you! Oh what a gooey mess!

As soon as Kenny has thrown the egg into the Audience, all four quickly put the carrier bags on their heads like hats and sing very fast indeed

All Four　　　　You have got some presents there
　　　　　　　　　　You have got some presents there

Act I, Scene 3

> You have got some presents there
> That—we—threw—out—to—you!!!
> Hey!

Black-out

Scene 3

The Ship's Galley

A simple insert set with practical porthole R *and a telephone* L—*the telephone could be collected from offstage. Upstage is a fairly big kitchen table with the required cooking props on it. Hanging down from above centre on a rope is a ship's lantern (not lit). By the table is a kitchen stool or a crate. (See scenery notes)*

Mrs Crusoe, wearing a small chef's hat or a mob cap, is singing loudly to herself as she sorts out the tins on the table

Bill and Ben enter

Bill You're the ship's cook so where's the grub? We're hungry!
Ben Will my spaghetti be long?
Mrs Crusoe How do I know? I haven't measured it.
Bill What about my chips?
Mrs Crusoe Chips? CHIPS? You've had your chips.
Ben And where are your dumplings?
Mrs Crusoe (*clutching her chest*) Cheeky thing.
Bill Well, what *are* you going to make for the crew?
Mrs Crusoe Would you like a chocolate sweetie?
Bill No, thank you, darling.
Mrs Crusoe In that case, while you two nautical nitwits are here you can help me get dinner ready for the crew.
Bill Great!
Mrs Crusoe All right then, help me with the table, there's a dear.

Bill and Ben bring the table down and thus Mrs Crusoe is standing behind it in position, directly under the ship's lantern

Mrs Crusoe (*pointing to the porthole*) Oh look! I wondered what it was. (*She collects a plastic bowl of dirty washing from the table, goes to the porthole, "opens" it and shoves all the laundry through*)
Ben Oh for heaven's sake, Mrs Crusoe, that's not a washing machine!
Bill It's a porthole! You can see the sea through it!
Mrs Crusoe Well I hope it doesn't get rough or I won't be able to cook the dinner. Ben, you go and see what the weather's like while I prepare things.

Mrs Crusoe straightens up the props on the table as Ben goes to the porthole and looks out

Ben (*importantly*) Right, you want a weather report and the weather is—ow!

Water is sloshed on Ben's face from offstage, and he reacts greatly, pretending that a huge amount of water has hit him

Mrs Crusoe (*to Bill*) What's the matter with him?
Bill I don't know.
Ben You don't know? I looked out of the window and a tidal wave hit me in the chops!
Bill Never!
Ben (*to the Audience*) Didn't a tidal wave hit me in the chops?
Audience Yes!
Ben There you are then!
Bill Nonsense. (*To the Audience*) You mean water came through the porthole and hit him?
Audience Yes!
Mrs Crusoe Go and have a look, Bill. I'm sure Ben's imagining it.
Bill Okay. (*He runs across to the porthole and looks out*) Nothing.

Bill goes back to the table and chats with Mrs Crusoe while Ben goes over to the porthole

Ben Nothing? Well I'm sure it was the sea water but I must be wrong! I thought I'd looked out of the porthole and a tidal wave had hit me and—ow!

Ben looks out of the porthole and receives the water again

Mrs Crusoe Now what's the matter with him?
Bill I don't know.
Ben (*wiping his face, making out he is absolutely drenched*) You don't know? It's the blooming tidal wave again!
Bill Never.
Ben (*coming downstage, to the Audience*) That was the tidal wave hitting me again, wasn't it?
Audience Yes!
Bill (*to the Audience*) You sure?
Audience Yes!
Bill (*to Ben*) Well, seeing's believing so I'll go over with you. Come on.

They both go to the porthole and look through

Nothing! I knew you were wrong! Let's have another look out.

They gaze out of the porthole

Mrs Crusoe (*laughing; to the Audience*) Poor old Ben! I'll tell you what's wrong with him. It's simple. He's what they call *accident prone* and—

The ship's lantern directly above Mrs Crusoe comes down and hits her head; there is a percussion crash and the lamp goes back again

OW!
Bill (*turning to Mrs Crusoe*) Did you call out?
Ben What's wrong, Mrs Crusoe?

Act I, Scene 3   21

Mrs Crusoe All I said was "He's accident prone"—and the lamp came down and bashed me on the bonce!
Bill and Ben (*laughing*) Don't be ridiculous.
Mrs Crusoe (*to the Audience*) It did, didn't it?
Audience Yes!
Bill ⎫
Ben ⎬ (*together*) Never!!
Mrs Crusoe It did! So I'm going to be careful while I cook—and we'd better get started. Now first, I want a little flour.

Bill picks up a red flower in a pot from the table and holds it up

You silly man. Not that sort of flour! I want *white* flour!

Ben picks up at his side of the table an identical pot flower with white petals

(*Fed up*) Doh! I'll do it myself. I'll get Charlie to send some up from the stores. (*She goes to the telephone and speaks into it*) Charlie, send up some flour as quick as you can!

Either talcum powder comes down the receiver or is blown on stage through a thin tube, off

OW! I didn't mean as quick as that, you twirp!

Ben and Bill laugh, Ben laughing so much that he staggers over to the porthole

Ben (*looking out*) Poor old Chrissie, covered in flour and—

Water is thrown over Ben again

Ow! (*He pretends he is drenched again*)
Bill (*seeing Ben*) Oh, not again!
Ben Yes again! (*To the Audience*) It was water, wasn't it?
Audience Yes!
Mrs Crusoe Well, maybe you did get the water, but we've got to get on and make the fish pie. Bill, get some fish from the fridge, there's a dear.
Bill Fish from the fridge!

Bill exits

Ben (*looking across at the porthole*) Every time I look out of the porthole the sea gets me. I can't understand it.
Mrs Crusoe I'll tell you what's wrong with you. It's simple. You're what they call *accident prone* and—

The ship's lantern comes down and hits her head—percussion crash—and goes up again

Ow!

Ben (*turning to Mrs Crusoe*) What's the matter?
Mrs Crusoe All I said was "You're accident prone"—and the lamp came down and bashed me on the bonce! (*To the Audience*) Didn't the lamp come down and bash me on the bonce?

Audience Yes!
Mrs Crusoe There you are, that's proof.

Bill enters, carrying a large plate with a cover on it. Underneath the cover is a large fish attached by a nylon wire to offstage

Hill Here's the fish!

Bill takes off the cover and the fish whizzes offstage on the wire with swanee whistle effect

Mrs Crusoe (*laughing*) Flying fish!
Ben Use the tin of sardines instead.
Mrs Crusoe All right. (*She holds up a sardine tin and dumps it in a plastic bowl*)
Bill (*putting his plate on the table and pointing to a bowl*) Is that the pastry?
Mrs Crusoe Yes, but it isn't moist enough.
Bill Oh, I'll put some water on it.
Mrs Crusoe All right, dear.
Ben And I'll put some pepper and salt on it.
Mrs Crusoe Good idea.

Ben picks up a large "pepper" pot (probably a plastic flour dredger) and shakes a cloud of "pepper" and does the same with a big salt container or packet — there are clouds everywhere

(*Laughing and choking*) That'll do! That's enough! And you, Bill, why haven't you put the water on the pastry?
Bill You mean do it right now?
Mrs Crusoe When do you think, you nitwit?
Bill But I don't know how to ...
Mrs Crusoe (*groaning*) Oh, for heaven's sake, use your head!

Bill shrugs, moves round the front of the table, faces upstage (thus masking himself) and bends down and revolves his head in the bowl

Getartoffit! You do it, Ben. You know how to pour water on pastry, don't you?
Ben (*blankly*) No.
Mrs Crusoe (*becoming really angry now*) Oh you're as bad as Bill. Can't you do anything for yourself? When I nod my head, pour the water over it!
Ben (*amazed*) What?
Mrs Crusoe When I nod my head, pour the water over it! And at once!

Mrs Crusoe nods her head, Ben quickly stands on the stool and pours a big jug full of water over her head

(*Spluttering; furiously*) Keep away from me, you two. Keep well away, you're driving me mad. (*She points* L) You, Bill, stand there. (*She points* R) And you, Ben, stand there. Keep well away from me. You're both impossible.
Bill ⎱
Ben ⎰ (*together*) Sorrreeeee!

Bill and Ben stand on either side of Mrs Crusoe, looking apologetic

Act I, Scene 4   23

Mrs Crusoe (*continuing her tirade*) I've never known such a fuss. All I want to do is make a fish pie! You know what's wrong with us three? No? I'll tell you. It's simple. (*Loudly*) We're what they call *accident prone!*

The lamp above her comes down and hits her—but also, there are two more lamps we haven't seen before. They now come down from the flies and Mrs Crusoe, Bill and Ben are all hit at the same moment—percussion crashes

All three (*shouting*) OW! HELP! NO!

There is a Black-out, accompanied by loud vaudeville music

SCENE 4

On the Poop Deck again

Tabs or frontcloth as before. (See production notes)

Sinister music. Dim lighting. Blackpatch enters with a lit lantern in one hand and a piece of hardboard in the other

Blackpatch Well, mateys, I've been watching that ship from my hideout down below. Now it's nightfall so it's time to signal!

The music simmers. Blackpatch holds up the hardboard in front of the lantern and signals towards the horizon

I—am—a—pirate—and—need—help. (*He gazes towards the horizon*) Curses, they haven't seen me! (*Overjoyed*) Yes, they have!

A signalling light comes back from the distant horizon. Blackpatch calls out the message

(*Slowly*) I—am—Jack—Boot.

There is a dramatic chord. Blackpatch is overjoyed

Jack Boot! Well, tickle me tonsils! We fought together with Captain Kidd! He's a mate o' mine, is Jack Boot! (*He starts to signal again*)

Polly enters behind Blackpatch

Polly Is that you, Robinson? (*Gasping*) Oh!

Polly runs back to the side of the stage to hide from Blackpatch

Blackpatch Attack—this—ship—when—we—reach—Tobago ...

The signal light replies

(*Reciting the reply*) Will—do—Wilco—and—out. (*He turns to the Audience and swings his lantern to and fro, laughing*)
    To take over this 'ere ship
    Twill soon be my pleasure

> Then we lands on Tobago
> And we digs up the treasure!
> Ha ha ha ha!

Blackpatch exits triumphantly

Polly runs out of hiding, puts cupped hands to her mouth and calls into the wings

Polly (*in a loud whisper*) Robinson, Robinson!

Robinson enters casually

Robinson Hello, Polly, what's the matter?
Polly We've got a pirate on board!
Robinson (*laughing*) Oh, Polly, you're always imagining things!
Polly It's true! (*To the Audience*) Isn't it true?
Audience Yes!
Robinson (*to the Audience*) You mean a *real pirate* on board?
Audience Yes!
Robinson (*to the Audience*) But who is he? ... He's who? Blackpatch?
Audience Yes!
Polly And Robinson, he signalled to a pirate ship and it's going to attack us!!
Robinson Then we must go and tell your father! Oh, just a minute—we must tell Captain Perkins to pretend *nothing is happening*—that will allay suspicion.
Polly Keep to the normal ship's routine?
Robinson Yes, but we'll tell him to alert everyone. Let the crew be secretly at the ready.
Polly All right. Robinson, I'm scared ...
Robinson No need to be! (*He sings*)

Song 7

Polly joins him in the duet

(*After the duet, romantically*) Polly, come over here for a moment ...

He takes her hand and they cross to the corner where Busby is

Audience BUSBY!

Kenny runs on

Kenny (*to the Audience*) Thanks, kids! (*To Robinson and Polly*) Hello, you two!
Robinson Kenny, we must warn you! There's a pirate on board!
Kenny (*excitedly*) OOOOooo!
Robinson He's trying to get his friends to attack the ship! But don't worry. I've still got the chart. He won't get it that easily.
Kenny Er ... could I borrow it for a minute?
Robinson Borrow it? I wouldn't dream of parting with it! We're going to brave rough seas, and tropical storms and even a pirate attack by what Polly was saying! (*He firmly clasps the chart to him*) It's going to show us the way to the treasure!

Act I, Scene 4

Polly Oh, Robinson ... He's your *brother*. He can borrow it for a few minutes surely?
Robinson Well ...
Polly You don't trust your own brother?
Robinson (*relenting*) I'm sorry, Kenny. Of course I trust you. (*He gives Kenny the chart*)
Polly You said we should warn Father.
Robinson (*anxiously*) Oh *yes!* (*To Kenny*) See you later—we've got to warn Captain Perkins about the pirates. Come on, Polly.

Robinson and Polly exit

Kenny (*holding up the chart; confused*) Now I've got it I don't know what to do with it. Any suggestions? (*Pointing to an imaginary person in the Audience*) Out! Common as muck, some people. No, I'm a bit fuzzy today, what shall I do with the chart?

Blackpatch enters

Blackpatch You'll give it to me, matey.
Kenny Will I, matey?
Blackpatch Yes, you will, matey.
Kenny But why should I give it to you? That's what I keep asking myself. I mean, you give things to people because you like them—

Blackpatch waves his arms at Kenny

Blackpatch   Abracadabra Abracadee
            Turn into a statue for me!

Kenny freezes into a statue

(*Taking the chart*) Thank you. (*Opening it*) Oh I can soon learn this by heart. (*Reading*) "The ruined temple is near the cannibal village. Walk ten paces East, six paces North ..."

He reads on while Kenny starts scratching and twitching as though the statue spell is making him uncomfortable, finally scratching his seat

Oh I've got that all right.

He rolls it up and puts it into Kenny's hand again

            So now I don't need the treasure chart
            'Cos I know the way to the treasure by heart!
            Ha ha ha!

Blackpatch exits

Kenny (*comically recovering from the spell*) OOoooo–aaaaaah — oh me back. (*He straightens up*) Oh, I do feel funny.

Robinson and Polly enter

Robinson Have you read the chart?
Kenny (*blankly*) What chart?

Robinson You're holding it in your hand. (*To Polly*) What's the matter with him?
Polly (*laughing*) He looks as though he's been hypnotized.
Robinson (*laughing*) Doesn't he?
Kenny Don't laugh at the afflicted, because I *have* been hypnotized. I'm serious.
Robinson What are you talking about?
Kenny I'll tell you ... It was like this. (*He takes a deep breath*) I was ...
Blackpatch (*at the offstage mike; or entering and exiting very quickly*)
>Abracadabra, Abracadee.
>Turn into a statue for me!

Kenny (*to the Audience*) I'm not telling them this time. (*With his arms outstretched, he turns right and starts to exit in a sleep-walker manner*)
Polly He's become gormless.
Robinson Oh no, he always looks like that.
Kenny (*almost at the exit, turning to the Audience*) What blooming cheek!

Kenny exits

Polly (*anxiously*) Robinson, there's something very strange going on.
Robinson Don't worry. I'll call the crew so that everyone's prepared. (*He blows several blasts on a whistle hanging round his neck*)

From each side the Sailors enter, the music of Song 8 starting

Robinson and Polly sing Song 8, the others joining in

Song 8

As the song begins, the tabs open or the frontcloth is flown and we are in

Scene 5

The Main Deck and the Mysterious Shipwreck

After the short vocal, some of the Sailors dance a hornpipe-style routine as the others clap in time

PRODUCTION ROUTINE

After the routine, all exit one side as the Captain enters the other. In this scene he needs to be aggressive

Captain (*calling*) Time for Mop Drill! Come on, you lazy landlubbers! Volunteers! Where are my volunteers? (*His striding about has caused him to reach Busby's corner*)
Audience Busby!

Kenny enters, calls out "Thanks kids!" while to more hornpipe music Mrs Crusoe (in uniform), Bill, Ben and perhaps a male singer (who looks as dopey as the others) shamble in and line up, chatting to each other

Act I, Scene 5

All (*ad libbing*) What's this about then? I was fast asleep in me bunk! Why is he shouting? What's he on about now?
Captain (*barking at them as they enter, his hands clasped behind his back*) You all know who I am, don't you?
Mrs Crusoe (*to the Audience*) Yes. Captain Bligh.
Captain I'm the Captain all right—and you're my crew and you're all here to do Mop Drill because this ship needs cleaning! It's filthy! What is it?
All It's filthy!
Captain Correct! (*To Kenny*) So the deck—the stem and the stern—mop it.
Kenny (*not concentrating*) What?
Captain Mop it!
Kenny (*enthusiastically*) Oh *yes*. Miss Piggy and Kermit and Ozzie and—
Captain Mop it, not Muppet! (*To the others*) All go and get some mops! (*As a command, shouted quickly*) Right turn!

Everyone, except Ben, turns right. Ben turns left

Left right, left right, left right, left right, left right!

They all, except Ben, march off fast and exit

Ben marches in the opposite direction

Captain Hey! You! You're going the wrong way!
Ben I'm going the *right* way—I'm trying to escape.
Captain Come back here!
Ben (*scared*) Yes, sir?
Captain I want discipline on board the *Mary Rose*. She's a fine ship with a fine motto. Recite the motto of the *Mary Rose*.
Ben Recite it?
Captain Yes.
Ben (*stupidly*) "Mary sat on a drawing pin. Mary rose."
Captain (*disgustedly*) Doh!

The others return, carrying mops, one of which is handed to Ben. As they fall in line Mrs Crusoe examines the top of her mop

Mrs Crusoe What a mess! It wants back combing! (*She "backcombs" the mop as though it is a head of hair*)
Captain Now—is the crew mustered?
Kenny (*overacting, as an "old sailor"*) I am. I'm hot, I am. I may be an old salt, but I'm mustered all right. Arrrrr. (*He salutes*)
Captain (*to all*) Look at you! You're all a complete shambles. What are you?
All A complete shambles.
Captain Louder!
All (*shouting*) A complete shambles!
Captain So pull yourselves together—close up!

Mrs Crusoe hands over her mop and lifts her skirt revealing white bloomers

What the devil are you doing? I mean the *other* way!
Mrs Crusoe Oh!

She turns round and lifts up her skirt again. On the seat of her white bloomers are two black hand marks made of black material sewn on

Captain What's the matter with you, you stupid woman?
Mrs Crusoe (*facing front again*) You said clothes up.
Captain I said clozzzzzzze up.
Mrs Crusoe (*to the Audience*) He said clozzzzzzze up. (*Conducting the others*) Right everybody.
All Clozzzzzzze up!
Captain (*to Mrs Crusoe*) And where on earth did you get that uniform?
Mrs Crusoe Mothercare.

Bill lifts one foot up, tucks the mop under his arm and hobbles forward as Long John Silver

Bill Oooooo—arrrrrrr—eeeeeee—arrrrrrr, Jim lad.
Captain Who d'you think you are?
Ben He thinks he's Long John Saliva. Arrr—eeee—rrrr—Jim lad.

The Captain takes away Bill's mop so that he falls down

Captain Shut up!
Mrs Crusoe Don't be nasty to him, Captain. He hasn't got a leg to stand on.

The Captain is becoming extremely impatient

Captain Get in line! Now you start mop drill with two taps on the deck, like this. (*He bangs the end of the mop handle on the deck twice*) Knock knock!
Bill Who's there?
Ben Toodle.
Bill Toodle who?
All Bye bye! Toodlehoo!

They all start to exit

Captain (*roaring*) Come back here! This is outrageous! I've never seen anything like it! Don't you realize I've been a regular for twenty-one years!
Mrs Crusoe (*to the Audience, with an American accent*) Thanks to Eno's Fruit Salts.
Captain I've never seen such a lousy lopsided load of lily-livered landlubbers.
Ben (*emotionally*) Oh, Captain, that's the nicest thing anyone's ever said to me. Thank you. I'm really moved. I'm proper choked. (*He sniffles and rubs his nose with his hand*)
The Others (*sympathetically*) Aaaah ...
Captain Silence! It's obvious that some of you have never set foot on the sea before! Why is that?
Bill Well if you set foot on the sea you fall in, you soppy thing!

They all laugh merrily

Sailor (*suddenly*) Please, sir, I've sailed with Drake!
Captain Sailed with Drake? You've never even sailed with a duck!

Act I, Scene 5

Sailor Oh, but I have. I've got a plastic duck in my bath at home. (*He steps forward and tells the Audience confidentially*) His name's Orville. (*He nods his head as though this is greatly important information*)
Captain (*sneering*) Orville? We need some organization round here. Now, call out your numbers in turn like proper sailors do! *Number!*

Ben is first in line and says nothing, Kenny calls out "two", Mrs Crusoe calls out "three", Bill calls out "four" and the sailor calls out "five"

Captain (*to the silent Ben*) You are one.
Ben (*reacting*) However did you guess?
Captain I give up. If you lot can't number, at least you can do the basic mop drill can't you? So watch this! Sloooo-ooope arms! (*He slopes arms with his mop and it rests on his shoulder*) Now all of you do it. (*Calling out the command*) Sloooo-ooope arms!

They energetically slope arms and thus throw the mops over their shoulders and they crash on to the floor behind them

Pick 'em up! Pick 'em up!

They pick up their mops

Right. We'll try that drill again. (*Commanding*) Sloooo-ooope arms!

They all watch him and manage to do it correctly except for Ben who has ended up with a mop on his left shoulder. The Captain is standing at Ben's right side

Not like that, you're going the wrong way.
Ben Oh, I see.

Ben swings round and his mop head hits the Captain's face

Captain (*spluttering*) No, no, look at Barnacle Bill next to you. You see where he's got his mop? Well, put yours there.
Ben Right.

Ben takes his mop and puts it on Bill's shoulder so that Bill now holds two

Bill (*defiantly*) I don't want to have two mops. I want to have one mop! It isn't fair!
Captain (*snatching the mop back and shoving it at Ben*) I'm determined that you shall all slope arms properly. (*Enraged*) I'm determined! (*He stamps his feet in fury*) I'm determined!
All (*stamping their feet and calling out with hysteria*) He's determined! He's determined!
Captain When there's the command "slope arms" all you have to do is this, you ignorant shower! (*Shouting*) One two three, *two* two three, and three! (*With fury he presents arms as he calls the command, and then throws away his mop on the floor in disgust*) So now ... SLOPE ARMS!
All One two three, *two* two three, and three! (*They do the movements — and also throw their mops away on the floor in disgust*)
Captain Pick 'em up! Pick 'em up! If you can't do that you'd better present arms! (*Sarcastically*) Do you know how to *present* arms?

All (*enthusiastically*) Oh *yes!* (*They all throw their mops at the Captain's feet*)
Captain Pick 'em up! Pick 'em up! Present arms but do it *properly!*

They collect the mops, move a little away and then turn to him with bows and curtsies and elegantly present the mops to him

    Take 'em back! Take 'em back and put 'em on your shoulders and get into line!

They get into line with the mops correctly on their shoulders

    Now!

This sudden shout is near Ben who jumps up in the air in fright

    Stand in line and march on the order! Left turn!

Kenny turns right

    What are you doing?
Kenny I'm not right, am I?
Captain No, you're right.
Kenny So if I want to do it right, I must turn left—right?
All Right!

Kenny faces the correct way

Captain And now we are going to march off very smartly, because now we are going to mop the mizzen deck.
Mrs Crusoe But it isn't there, Captain!
Captain Why not?
Mrs Crusoe It's mizzen.

They all laugh at this, and turn to each other with ad libs like "That was good, wasn't it?" "Isn't Chrissie Crusoe a comic?" (etc)

Captain Stand still! We are going to march away to the mizzen deck whether it's mizzen or not! So get ready—
All (*shouting*) Get ready!
Captain Get set—
All (*shouting*) Get set!
Captain Go!
All Go, go!

They all loudly sing "La da da da da" to "A Life on the Ocean Wave" as they march round the stage and exit

The stage is empty. The Lights fade down and sinister music is heard

    Blackpatch enters

Blackpatch Now is the time for all good men to come to the aid of the party—arrrrrr! (*He creeps across the stage and signals over the ship's side by whistling*)

There is a reply whistle

Act I, Scene 5

Blackpatch helps Jack Boot aboard, over the bulwarks

Jack Boot!
Jack Boot Blackpatch, me old mate!
Blackpatch ⎫
Jack Boot ⎭ *(together, embracing)* Arrrrrrr!
Blackpatch *(breaking away)* Sssssh! We must keep quiet, this be a surprise attack. Are all your brave lads ready?
Jack Boot Aye! *(Beckoning over the ship's side)* Ready, willing and able!

From over the bulwarks and from the nearby wings the extremely ferocious looking Pirates enter, waving bottles of rum, and daggers, swords and guns. As they enter on tip toe to the tingling music and creep about, they address the Audience

1st Pirate *(loudly)* So this is Robinson Crusoe's ship!
2nd Pirate *(loudly)* I'll cut his gizzard!
3rd Pirate *(loudly)* I'll throttle his wind-pipe!
Jack Boot What we want is a nice juicy murder!
Blackpatch Quietly, me darlings, quietly, sssssh!
All Ssssssh!

They look at each other, fingers to lips. They form an extremely menacing and bloodthirsty line across the footlights, in various caricature versions of Errol Flynn heroic pirate poses, waving daggers, guns, swords and baring their teeth, sneering, clawing the air

You may want Bill and Ben to also enter here, to swell the Pirate horde, because as every Pirate wears a black patch over his eye plus huge earrings, headscarf (etc) the Audience cannot see through the disguise—the quick change is easily done

There is a fanfare, and the Pirates sing at the tops of their voices. Either it is partly a solo for Blackpatch, or another Pirate can sing the Blackpatch lyric. However arranged Blackpatch sings his lines fairly quietly, and the others sing double forte

Song 9—With Cat-Like Tread

When all sing "Yah" everyone stamps their feet and there is a thunderously loud crash from percussion and a noisy chord from the band. The song is presented in gutsy pantomime, not operetta, style

Blackpatch	With cat-like tread
All	Yah!
Blackpatch	Upon our prey we steal
All	Yah!
Blackpatch	In silence dread
All	Yah!
Blackpatch	Our cautious way we feel!
All	Yah!
Blackpatch	No sound at all (Yah!)

All (*quieter*)	We never speak a word (Yah!) A fly's footfall Would be distinctly heard! So stealthily the pirate creeps While all the household softly sleeps Oooooo—oooooo—oooooo

Then all sing with gusto:

>Come friends who sail the sea
>Be an artful dodger
>Fly the Jolly Roger
>Let's add some burglaree
>To our wicked piracee!

They reprise these five lines with even more gusto. Then into the following Blackpatch solo. (This solo is optional, or can be swaggeringly spoken instead of sung)

Song 9(a)

Blackpatch	Oh I shall live and I shall die Under the brave black flag I fly And I shall play a villainous part With a pirate head and a pirate heart I'll hide away in a pirate creek And sink a couple of ships a week I'll blow them up as this song I sing And live and die a Pirate King! For I am a Pirate King—
All	You are—hurrah for our Pirate King!
Blackpatch	And it is, it is a glorious thing To be a Pirate King!
All	Hurrah—hurrah for our Pirate King!!!

Towards the end of this number Jack Boot collects from the wings a large skull and cross-bones flag on a pole which he hands to Blackpatch who stands centre stage, waving the flag. The Pirates kneel each side and point at it in a Grand Tableau on the last notes, which end with a cheer

Pirates Hurrah!

After the number, Blackpatch and Jack Boot put fingers to lips

Blackpatch \
Jack Boot } (*together*) Ssssssh!

Led by Blackpatch they all creep upstage, and examine the ship

   Downstage Robinson enters, sword in hand, leading on his fighting crew

Robinson (*shouting and waving his sword*) Have at you!

THE PIRATE FIGHT

All are involved both comically and seriously—see production notes at end of script. Finally, two of the fighters cross down to Busby's corner as they fight

Act I, Scene 5

Audience Busby!

Kenny runs in and calls out above the noise "Thanks, kids!" He is wearing football referee gear. He blows his whistle and sternly orders the Pirates off

Kenny (*pointing*) Off!
All (*pointing*) Off!

Everyone, except Blackpatch, Robinson and two members of the Chorus, exit—the victors escorting the defeated Pirates

The two Chorus members tie Blackpatch to the mast

Robinson (*pointing his sword at Blackpatch*)
    It's best to have you tied up here
    'Cos the Island of Tobago's near
    If you try to escape it will be the end
    Yes, it'll be curtains for you, my friend!

Robinson and the Chorus members exit

Blackpatch (*to the Audience*) Who does he think he is, the cheeky brat? I'll get my own back on him somehow, mateys—What I want is REVENGE!

Polly enters from the opposite side to which Robinson left

At once Blackpatch starts to moan piteously

Blackpatch Oh ... woe ... oh ...
Polly (*calling*) Robinson! When does the ship—
Blackpatch (*struggling and groaning piteously*) Aaaah ... ooooh ...
Polly What's the matter, Blackpatch?
Blackpatch Have pity on me. The ropes are so tight.
Polly Oh no, I'm not falling for that one.
Blackpatch If you could loosen them a *bit!*
Polly No.
Blackpatch Please.
Polly No. (*She starts to go*)
Blackpatch Then would you read to me?
Polly (*surprised*) *Read* to you??
Blackpatch It's a book I have. A book of nursery rhymes.
Polly Well ... is that the book in your belt?
Blackpatch Yes, matey ... You are kind. Bless you.

Polly takes the book from Blackpatch's belt and opens it

    Could you turn to the letter E?
Polly Letter E ... (*She turns the pages*)
Blackpatch Then—it's only a little nursery rhyme—will you read out the page?
Polly (*frowning*) I'm not sure ... (*To the Audience*) Is there something strange about this book?
Audience Yes!
Polly Is it a nursery rhyme book?
Audience No—magic! (*etc*)

Polly Magic? (*Laughing*) Oh no, I don't think it's that! I mean listen to this. (*She reads innocently*)
"E stands for Earwig or something far worse
E stands for Egypt and the Pyramid's Curse
Abracadabra and Abracadee
E for Escape—and I now set you free!"

There is a dramatic chord. Blackpatch's bonds become "free" and he throws them away

(*Gasping*) It *was* magic!
Blackpatch Yes, it was magic, me dear. (*He takes a dagger from his belt*) And now you can do me another "good turn". You can turn to the letter "S".

She turns the pages then hands the book to him, terrified

Polly But what does the letter S stand for?
Blackpatch Letter S? SHIPWRECK! (*He reads aloud*)
"Signs of the Zodiac, one, two, three,
Evil Spirits now harken to me
Come ye forth from the mighty deep
From the oil and slime you creep..."

The lighting flickers and the stage darkens

Polly (*terrified*) Robinson, Robinson, help me!

Robinson runs on

Robinson What's the matter?

Polly points to Blackpatch, and Robinson gasps

Blackpatch free! And what's that black ship? (*He points off*)
Blackpatch That "black ship" is what we villains likes to call an "oil tanker", matey.
Polly (*scared, as she looks off*) It's an evil-looking ship!
Robinson (*anxiously*) There's a banner being waved! And on the banner, it says "W.C."!
Blackpatch Yes—'tis a flag of convenience!
Robinson (*terrified*) A flag of convenience! Oh no!

There is a dramatic chord. Polly runs to Robinson, who holds her to him

Polly Stop him, Robinson—stop him!
Robinson (*gallantly*) Yes!
Blackpatch No. 'Cos this is where I put you two mateys under my spell. (*He waves his arms at them and recites*)
I've sailed on great big galleons
I've sailed on a little skiff
And now you two rapscallions—
May your feet be frozen stiff!!

There is a crash from percussion, both Robinson and Polly cry out and try to move their feet but they are "stuck to the floor"

Act I, Scene 5

Blackpatch turns to the Audience

> My slimy friends will sink this ship
> You're powerless to stop 'em
> Soon the oil will stick to the sides
> And drag the boat to the bottom!

Robinson (*trying to move from his position*) I can't move!
Polly Neither can I!
Robinson We're trapped!

They struggle but still their feet seem stuck to the ground

Blackpatch (*calling loudly*) BEHOLD—DEMON OYLSLICK!

Gurgling sounds are heard, accompanied by slow, turgid, gooey music

Demon Oylslick slowly rises up from the side of the ship and stands, posed, for his dramatic announcement

Oylslick   Yes, I am Demon Oylslick
> The curse of the seven seas
> I strike fear in the heart of man
> For I do what I please!
> Now the oil tanker breaks in two
> And that's the end of your friends and you!

He waves his arms to offstage. There is a crash from percussion. Oylslick becomes hysterical with delight

> Human beings are made my slaves!
> With oil from the tanker all over the waves!
> Oil! Oil! Oil!

Oylslick waves his arms about and the Oil Minions slither aboard

Robinson and Polly try to move but are unable to. The Minions claw at the rigging and sails which slowly fall, they slowly claw at the mast which falls sideways, and over the side they bring a "blanket" of black oily seaweed and they choreographically swamp the ship in oil. (See production notes.) We hear oil gurgling and sucking sounds. Blackpatch looks about him, much pleased and stands centre stage. Oylslick is near him, still casting spells about the scene

Blackpatch We'll sink this ship, Demon Oylslick and me
> Down to the depth of the slimy sea!
> Ha ha ha!

The lighting fades to just a spot on the laughing Blackpatch and Oylslick, who is crouched beside him waving his arms about in a slimy sinister way. Oylslick moves downstage and the tabs close behind him or a frontcloth is flown in

Scene 6

Demon Oylslick's gruesome Grotto

Tabs or frontcloth of darkly sinister rocks and seaweed with horizontal streaks of blue to suggest it is under the sea

The action is continuous, Oylslick continuing his slimy movements. It is effective if there is a slow drum beat or "wire brush" percussion effect under his speech, as he rubs his hands slowly together with delight

Oylslick   Everywhere my wickedness
And evil villainy reaches!
Everywhere my oily sludge
Is on your sandy beaches!
When I command, my Minions obey
And thus we destroy your summer holiday!
My hour of triumph
You will not begrudge
'Cos there's nothing more foul
And filthy than sludge!
Yeuk!
Ha ha ha ha ha!

A few bars of glissando music as the Sea Fairy enters from the right. With much confidence she addresses the Audience

Fairy   I see he's standing on the stage
And in the very centre
But I'm the Detergent Fairy—
MY NAME IS DETERGENTA!

Oylslick   If you think that you can conquer
Then, Fairy, you are daft!
My Minions have dragged Robinson
Crusoe from his raft!

Oylslick slinks about as he speaks, continually waving his arms, yet the Fairy remains greatly confident

Fairy   But I come from a *shining* place
Where all is sweetness and light
Where the bright blue waves are *really* blue
And the white is dazzling white!
When things look black and the matter's urgent
What you need is a bit of detergent!
So I'll rescue Robinson Crusoe
This promise I'll soon prove—

An aside to the Audience as though a television commercial

Act I, Scene 6   37

| | And look at my lovely hands, my dears,
| | So soft and white and smooth!
| **Oylslick** | Huh!
| | You say you'll rescue Robinson—
| | Just how are you going to do so?
| | Stuck fast in my gruesome grotto
| | Is your hero Robinson Crusoe!
| | He and his girl friend, Polly
| | To an oil slick they are pinioned
| | Held by my ghastly, greasy, gooey,
| | Gurgling, oily Minions!
| **Fairy** | It isn't true, you can't fool me!
| **Oylslick** | It isn't true? Just watch and see!

(*He makes slimy magic passes to the wings*)

To dramatic music Robinson and Polly, now with strips of black plastic draped over them like a sort of cloak, are dragged on stage left by the Minions who group around them making smothering-style gestures

> Against me, Robinson Crusoe
> You never had a chance!
> For now the Demon Oylslick
> Will lead you quite a dance!

The Minions claw and stroke at Robinson and Polly as the percussion and "sludgy" music continues

Polly Save me, Robinson!
Robinson I can't! Help us, somebody, help!

The Fairy urgently addresses the Audience

| **Fairy** | Something must be done, my dears
| | And done now, very quick.
| | 'Cos there's nothing more revolting
| | Than a horrible oil slick!
| | Yes, this is where we take up arms
| | Against a sea of troubles—
| | I'm not the Detergent Fairy for nothing
| | Behold—my Magic Bubbles!

She waves her wand towards the wings L. *Oylslick looks off and gasps melodramatically with horror pointing to where bubbles start to drift on stage. (See production notes)*

| **Oylslick** | The antidote! Farewell to Oil
| | And Sludge and Kerosene!
| **Fairy** | Oh yes, my Demon Oylslick,
| | THIS will make you come clean!
| **Robinson** } (*together*) Thank you, good Fairy!
| **Polly** |

Robinson and Polly laugh and exit triumphantly together. The music continues as the Minions see the bubbles, point to them, react with horror and, gasping as though out of breath and dying, they exit. Oylslick himself makes a grand melodramatic, staggering exit

Oylslick (*gasping as he goes*) Detergent! Detergent bubbles! Agh!

Oylslick goes

Fairy   And now here in this grotto
                     I warn you to be wary
                     I'll call on the Fairy Liquid—
                     My friend, the Liquid Fairy!

She becomes a Fairy version of a Victorian Music Hall Chairman, as she delivers her spiel

Good Mortals, it is time for you to be tittilated by a tremendous underwater entertainment! May I proudly present those subaqueous stars, those under the sea sensations, those delightful dancers, those balletic bombshells ... (*Magnificently*) Yes, it's Rudy Near Enough and Dame Margot Fountain!

She waves her wand, music from "Swan Lake" bursts forth and the Tabs open or the frontcloth is flown and we are at

Scene 7

The "Mary Rose", now under the sea

The ship is now in a transformation scene style setting as the oil effects have been replaced by cut-outs of attractive sea shells and seaweed. This can be quickly done—see scenery notes

At once, Kenny enters as a comedy version of a classical male ballet dancer, soon followed by Mrs Crusoe also in balletic attire

The Fairy exits

Music 10—Short "cod" ballet

See production notes. After the dance Mrs Crusoe and Kenny bow and curtsey extravagantly and exit

The Fairy enters

Fairy (*to the Audience*) Robinson Crusoe's ship may have been wrecked, but it is near the shore, so I can easily save him with the help of my attendant sea sprites! (*She waves her wand*)

The Sea People enter or just the Minions return

Act I, Scene 7

Music 11—Short dance routine

Fairy (*after the dance*)
> This place is near the desert island
> So now to help Robinson get to *dry* land!

There is a fanfare and all form a tableau

> Robinson, in his Transformation Scene cloak, enters on a Dolphin carriage drawn by juveniles dressed as sea horses, or with cut-outs of dolphins. (See scenery notes)

> My carriage is drawn by dolphins and they will take you to your desert island!

Robinson (*declaiming*) To the Desert Island! *To the Treasure of Tobago!*

Robinson and all on stage reprise the last eight bars of

Song 5 (reprise)

On the last note, there is a Grand Tableau

Note: Either the Sea People can wear "ponchos" over their Sailor/Pirate costumes, or they do not enter at all for this Interval Tableau

CURTAIN

ACT II

Scene 1

On the shore of the desert island of Tobago

Before the CURTAIN *rises loud drum beats and cannibal shouts of "Boola! Boola!" are heard. The* CURTAIN *rises on a palm-tree-lined seashore (see scenery notes)*

The Cannibals are dancing a noisy and energetic routine. As they dance and shuffle and wave their spears they call out bloodcurdling shouts of "Baboossa! Yambessi!" and "Boola!" (which is the cannibal catchphrase)

Song 12

After the routine everyone reacts as they hear someone approach

The Cannibals exit to hide themselves

Robinson enters in his legendary "desert island" costume, a rifle slung on his shoulder

Robinson I've walked about for hours on this shore, remembering that all my comrades are drowned . . . (*He pats the rifle*) I've rescued my trusty rifle from the shipwreck and with it some ammunition. (*He pats the belt pouch*) But after the various exertions, I'm tired . . .

He kneels down at the footlights with a heavy sigh—which stops abruptly. He stares at the ground. We hear tingle effects from percussion

(*Dramatically*) A footprint! Then there *are* others on this island! Perhaps some of my friends are saved after all! (*Curiously*) But this is the print of a *bare* foot, a large foot . . .

Drumbeats are heard

(*To the Audience*) Drumbeats! Are they natives . . . (*He says this next as a highly unlikely joke, not smiling*) . . . or are they cannibals?
Audience Cannibals!
Robinson (*not smiling*) Cannibals? You sure?
Audience Yes!
Robinson (*taking the gun from his shoulder*) Then I must hide! (*Apprehensively*) Cannibals . . .

Robinson exits stealthily

The drumbeats at once grow louder and louder until double forte

Act II, Scene 1

A terrified Man Friday runs across the stage, looking wildly about him
Friday (*shouting*) Mabayo! Balloossu mabayo! (*Petrified, he runs to and fro*)
The Cannibals enter with shields and spears
The Cannibals grab Friday
There is a dramatic chord as Wotta Woppa the impressive and fierce Cannibal Queen enters, shouting commands at the others
Wotta Woppa (*waving her arm in salute*) Yamoossa! Boola!
Cannibals (*saluting her with their spears*) Yamoossa! Boola!
Wotta Woppa Yamoossa talooba! Yamoossa *moonda* talooba! (*To the Audience, threateningly*) Mah name is Wotta Woppa! Yes, Ah is Wotta Woppa da cannibal queen and (*pointing to the terrified Friday*) he is a load of old rubbish! (*To the others*) Dis stupid man heyah, he have da nerve to tell me dat being a cannibal is wicked!
Cannibals (*furiously, sympathizing with her*) Boola! Boola!
Wotta Woppa (*to the Audience, greatly incensed*) He have da nerve to tell me dat Ah must only eat vegetables! Ah say to him "Vegetables? Yeuk!"
Cannibals Vegetables—yeuk!
Wotta Woppa (*to Friday*) For insulting me an' ma cannibal way of life, you shall die, you—you *vegetarian*. (*To a nearby cannibal*) William, shake spear!
1st Cannibal (*waving spear*) Boola!
Wotta Woppa Dat's it! (*Commanding*) Umballa goodoo badwana!

She points to the carved totem pole and they drag the struggling Friday to the pole and tie him there. The drumbeats have been continuous and now become very loud while there are shouts and all threaten Friday by waving their spears at him

Cannibals (*ad lib shouting*) Gambeeda! Yamoossoo! Zambossa! Dombi—dombi! (*They lean forward and pull faces at him*)

Wotta Woppa takes from her belt a long knife and holds it above the shaking and terrified Friday's chest

Wotta Woppa (*ready to strike downwards*) And a one, and a two, and a—

Robinson enters and watches horrified

As Wotta Woppa is about to strike Robinson shouts out

Robinson STOP! Now I'll scare the life out of you bloodthirsty lot! (*He takes the gun from his shoulder and deliberately aims at the sky*)

There is a loud bang (off) and the Cannibals and Wotta Woppa freeze with terror, let out a series of yells and run off

Robinson blows across the barrel of the gun

We'll soon set you free, my friend!

Putting down the rifle Robinson runs forward, stands in front of Friday and takes out a knife from his belt and sets Friday free

Well, that's that. I don't know what those villains think they're up to because—

He looks around and cannot see Friday. Friday is on the ground at his feet bowing down low, and jabbering with fear

Where are you? Oh, there you are! (*Realizing*) Great Heavens, don't bow like that! I'm only Robinson Crusoe!

He lifts Friday up. Friday stands there shivering

Friday Yuh—yuh—yuh—yuh.
Robinson Why you're trembling all over! I won't hurt you!
Friday (*still terrified*) Boola! Boola! (*He mimes Robinson firing the gun*) BANG!
Robinson (*explaining*) No. It's all right. I'm your *friend!*

Friday shivers

He doesn't understand. (*To Friday*) I'm not one of those cannibals, and neither are you! We can relax—laugh together—ha ha ha ha!

There is no reaction from Friday, so he tries again

Ha ha ha!

Friday (*with a small tentative laugh*) Ha ha.

Robinson nods encouragingly, Friday decides Robinson is safe so he laughs a bit more

Ha ha ha!

Friday becomes relaxed and laughs with relief a great loud laugh

Oh—ha ha ha!!!!

Friday takes off a wooden bead necklace and hands it to Robinson

Robinson (*emotionally*) Why ... thank you!

Friday beams, this gesture has been a success

Thank you very much in fact!

Robinson shakes Friday's hand. Friday enjoys this and pumps Robinson's hand up and down violently, over and over

Help, that's enough! You'll pull my arm off! You don't speak English do you?
Friday Boola!
Robinson Well, it's nice to meet you!

Friday just stares at Robinson who begins to feel embarrassed

(*Chatting fatuously*) Well, I come from (*a local place—somewhere that*

Act II, Scene 1

sounds ridiculous). Er—it's near (*another local name*). Oh dear, this is hopeless. (*He points at Friday and speaks distinctly*) What—is—your—name?

Friday thinks Robinson is pointing offstage so he turns round and starts to exit

Hey! Come back. (*He waves Friday back. Pointing to himself*) Me Crusoe.
Friday (*pointing to himself*) Me ... Crusoe.
Robinson No, no, *me* Crusoe.
Friday (*emphatically*) ME Crusoe.
Robinson (*giving up*) Oh, blimey.
Friday Oh, blimey.
Robinson Me Crusoe and you—well—I don't know what to call you. Some name like Moowga. Mr Moowga?
Friday (*with a big smile*) Boola.
Robinson (*pulling a face*) Boola? I can't call you "Boola!" (*To the Audience*) He's a bit like a Jamaican man, isn't he, man, with that smile, man, OK, man? I know I'll just call you "Man". (*To Friday*) Man.
Friday Bam.
Robinson No, *Man*.
Friday (*repeating the inflections*) No, *Man*.
Robinson (*shouting*) MAN!
Friday (*shouting loudly*) MAN! MAN! MAN!
Robinson That's right! Well, I'm Robinson Crusoe so I'd better call you Man Crusoe—no, that's not right ... The month is January so I could call you Man January ... (*To the Audience*) I don't like any of these names, so any ideas?
Audience Man Friday!
Robinson Man Heidi? That's a girl's name, Heidi!
Audience Man Friday!
Robinson Man *FRIDAY!* Oh that's good! You mean call him Friday because today is Friday—I like that! Thanks! Great! (*To Friday*) You Friday!
Friday (*pointing to himself*) Friday?
Robinson Yes. (*Nodding enthusiastically, encouraging him*) Try it out, Friday!

Friday tries out the name

Friday (*ordinary voice*) Friday. (*Deep voice*) Friday. (*High voice*) Friday. (*Squeezed throat voice*) Friday. (*He starts to do a sort of jive*) Friday—Friday—Friday—yeah! (*He moves all over the stage shouting*) Friday! Friday! Friday!
Robinson That's great! Except it's getting to be an elocution lesson! (*He snaps his fingers*) That's it! *Elocution lesson!* (*To Friday*) "The rain in Spain".
Friday Boola.
Robinson Oh dear. "*The rain*".
Friday (*getting it right*) De rain.
Robinson (*hugely excited*) YES, FABULOUS! (*Very slowly*) "The rain in Spain lies mainly in the plain."

Friday Boola!
Robinson Now stop it, Friday, you're not trying. Come on. "The rain in Spain lies mainly in the plain."
Friday De ray in Spay lie may in the play.
Robinson Very good! Excellent!
Friday (*jumping in the air; laughing*) Excellent, Friday! Excellent, Friday! Yeah!
Robinson Once more, best of all, *try really hard*, you're doing fabulously...

Friday concentrates very hard, pulling comical faces and suddenly speaks in a slow and very la-di-da accent indeed

Friday The rain in Spain lies mainly in the plain.
Robinson (*delighted*) Friday, that's fantastic! I can see we're to be great friends! (*He sings Song 13*)

Song 13

Soon Friday joins in, pronouncing the words in an odd way and maybe he can't sing very well

After their duet and short dance, Robinson and Friday exit

Mrs Crusoe enters in a ship-wrecked costume

Mrs Crusoe (*gazing round*) Oh, so *this* is Southend! (*To the Audience*) We're all on a desert island—we're macarooned! (*She moves downstage*) Oh, I've found another footprint! (*She picks up a white shoe lining from the footlights and sighs deeply*) Poor sole...

Bill enters, gazing round, and the band plays a few bars of "A Sleepy Lagoon"

Bill Hullo, Mrs Crusoe!
Mrs Crusoe What are you looking for? This is a desert island.
Bill Roy Plomley! No, I'm looking for a drink if you want to know, I'm longing for a bit of refreshment—it's so hot! Maybe there's some juicy pineapples or something...
Mrs Crusoe Oh, you don't need pineapples!
Bill I don't?
Mrs Crusoe No! All you have to do is play a little game.
Bill Oh, I like playing games. What do I have to do?
Mrs Crusoe (*demonstrating*) Shut your eyes, hold out your hands and say "Busy Bee, Busy Bee, what have you got in the hive for me?" Then you open your eyes and I'll give you the refreshment.
Bill That's amazing! (*Pleased*) Thanks, Mrs Crusoe!
Mrs Crusoe (*starting to flap her arms as though they were wings and making buzzing noises*) Buzzz-zzz. (*Explaining*) I'm a stupid old bee.
Bill I could have told you that.

Mrs Crusoe exits, buzzing and flapping, into the wings

Bill, unawares, chats to the Audience

Act II, Scene 1   45

What a nice woman, not another like her in the whole world. And she worked and slaved to make ends meet when Robinson and Kenny were kids...

Mrs Crusoe comes back again with her mouth full of water

Oh, here she is back again! What was the little rhyme she asked me to say! Oh yes... (*To Mrs Crusoe*) "Busy Bee, Busy Bee, what have you got in the hive for me?

Mrs Crusoe squirts water at Bill and laughs

Mrs Crusoe (*convulsed*) Oh dear! You should see... oh... Bill, you should see yourself... oh... it... I... you... oh!

Laughing helplessly Mrs Crusoe staggers off and exits one side as Ben enters the other

Bill (*wiping his face*) Ah! Here comes Ben Dover! He's been annoying me a lot lately. This is where I get my own back. (*Cheerfully*) Hullo, Ben!
Ben What's the matter with your face?
Bill I've been running for a bus. My face is covered in Presbyterian. Well, it's hot isn't it?
Ben Oh, it is, I'm dying for some refreshment.
Bill (*eagerly*) You are? Then all you have to do is shut your eyes, hold out your hands and say "Busy Bee, Busy Bee, what have you got in the hive for me?" then open your eyes and I'll give you the refreshment.
Ben (*pleased*) Oh, thanks, Bill—that's marvellous! All I have to do is shut my eyes and hold out my hands—like this.
Bill That's right! (*To the Audience*) Oh, it's a crying shame. His sailor's uniform will get soaking wet, poor soul. (*To Ben*) I must buzz off now and get the refreshment... Buzz, zzz... (etc)

Bill exits flapping arms and buzzing

Ben What a good idea! He's a grand person is Bill. (*Sentimentally*) Bill the Bosun—I wouldn't go on a voyage without him. (*To the Audience*) Now what was the rhyme?
Audience "Busy Bee, Busy Bee, what have you got in the hive for me?"
Ben That's right, thanks! (*Looking off*) Ah, here he comes now.

Bill enters flapping his arms and making buzzing noises and then stands by Ben with his mouth full of water

(*Reciting*) "Busy Bee, Busy Bee, I'll have my tea at half past three."

There is silence from Bill but an encouraging look suggests "try again"

Well, don't look at me like that—you asked me to say the poem and I have. "Busy Bee, Busy Bee, I'll have my tea at half past three."

Bill is compelled to swallow with a great gulp

Bill No, no, you nitwit. It's "Busy Bee, Busy Bee, what have you got in the hive for me?" or it doesn't work. I'll nip off and you try again.

Bill exits with arms flapping and buzzing noises

Ben I must remember that rhyme. Trouble is I haven't got a very good memory. I know what it is! (*Reciting*) "Mary had a little lamb, it's fleece ..." (*The Audience has interrupted*) What should it be then?
Audience "Busy Bee, Busy Bee, what have you got in the hive for me?"
Ben Oh, of course. Thanks! Here he comes.

Bill returns with arms flapping and stands next to Ben, his mouth full of water

I've got it now. I had the inflections wrong last time. It should be *bus* . . . y bee, *bus* . . . y bee, er . . . er . . . well I've got the first part right! (*Trying to remember*) *Bus* . . . y bee, *bus* . . . y bee . . . er . . . er . . .

Bill gulps down the water

Bill (*slapping Ben*) Shut up!
Ben Sorry, I was only trying—
Bill What's up with you?
Ben I was only trying. I forgot.
Bill Ach, a child could remember it. "Busy Bee, Busy Bee, what have you got in the hive for me?"
Bill I'll remember it this time. I'm not an idiot, you know.
Bill You could have fooled me.

Bill exits flapping and making buzzing noises

Ben mumbles to himself, trying to remember the rhyme

Ben "Busy Bee, Busy Bee, you've got honey so have we."

The Audience will correct him and shout out the correct words

Bill returns. But on his way to Ben he trips up and is thus forced to expel the water

Ben "Busy Bee, Busy Bee," (*innocently*) did you have a nice trip?
Bill Shut up!
Ben Don't shout at me. I'm only trying to remember it. What happened then?
Bill I was looking for the honey for you, you dolt.
Ben Oh, I see.
Bill I'll go and have another look.
Ben All right!
Bill (*wearily*) I'll go and get it but I'm a very tired little bee now.

Bill exits, wearily flapping his arms and buzzing

Ben mumbles to himself furiously trying to remember the words and this time pulling amazing faces as he concentrates. The Audience will shout out the correct words, and he nods his thanks to them, and continues to pull faces as he mutters

Bill enters and stands by Ben with his mouthful of water

Bill sees Ben pulling faces, starts to laugh and to his dismay swallows the water

Act II, Scene 1

(*Exasperated*) It's "Busy Bee, Busy Bee, what have you got in the hive for me!"—and stop pulling faces and making me laugh!!

Bill exits quickly, buzzing and arms flapping

Ben I'm all right now. He's just this minute said the rhyme to me, so I'm all right this time.

Bill enters with a mouthful of water and stands by Ben

"Oh, Busy Bee, if you will be so kind, do you think you could spare a drop of water?"

Bill makes encouraging signs that become frantic

That's it! I've said it! "Oh, Busy Bee, if you would be so kind, do you think you could ..."

Bill (*swallowing the water*) Shut up!!

Ben I'm sorry. I made up my own version and it wasn't right, was it? Now, if I could just—

Bill (*furiously*) I'm not running to and fro all day looking for honey for you! This is your last chance! Please, do it right this time, otherwise I warn you, I shall throw a tantrum.

Ben You throw what you like, as long as it misses me.

Bill (*tearfully*) If you forget this time—if you forget—oh, just say anything at all!

Ben All right, I will.

Bill exits

Ben takes a small flask from his pocket and fills his mouth with water

Bill returns

Bill and Ben gaze at each other. Then Bill makes encouraging gestures but instead of replying Ben makes the same gesture back. Bill makes fiercer and more urgent gestures back. Now their cheeks become very blown out as they stand there. They remain staring at each other with an occasional gesture. At last, Bill is the one to admit defeat and is compelled to spurt out the water

Bill But it's so easy! I don't know what's the matter with you! It works every time! Don't you realize, you stupid illiterate fool, that all you have to say is (*slowly and condescendingly*) "Busy Bee, Busy Bee, what have you got in the hive for me?"

At this Ben squirts out the water into Bill's face. Bill is enraged. Loud vaudeville music is heard

Black-out

In the black-out we hear drum beats or sinister music

Scene 2

The Cannibal Village and Stewpot
Tabs, or frontcloth of native huts in a jungle clearing
Sinister music is heard. Blackpatch and Jack Boot (holding a gun) enter laughing loudly and boastfully together. The drum beats fade down

Blackpatch (*nostalgically*) Ah, Jack Boot, me old darlin', remember when we boarded that ship and grabbed all the women!
Jack Boot Arr! Once aboard the lugger and the girl is mine!
Blackpatch Always up to some wicked scheme, bain't we, matey? (*Confidentially*) As for *this* wicked scheme, we've got to get the Cannibal Queen on our side, see?
Jack Boot (*nodding*) I'm with 'eee all the way, Cap'n.
Blackpatch Then she can show us the way to the hidden treasure, see?
Jack Boot You're as crafty as Captain Kidd! (*He rubs his hands together*)
Blackpatch Aye, she can take us to the Ruined Temple, 'cos that's where the treasure's buried, matey! (*He laughs boisterously*) Ha! Ha! Ha!
Jack Boot (*laughing boisterously, echoing Blackpatch*) Ho ho ho! We'll be rich beyond the Dreams of Avocado! Oh, Cap'n, everything you do is a success—from port to starboard! Ha ha ha!
Blackpatch From the rigging to the rudder! Ho ho ho!

Blackpatch thinks this is so funny that he staggers over to the corner where Busby's cage hangs

Audience Busby!

Kenny enters the other side to the pirates and calls out cheerfully to the Audience

Kenny Thanks, kids! I wondered if Busby was all right and now— (*He sees the Pirates and is terrified, putting his hand to his mouth*) Oh, cripes! (*He listens to them*)
Blackpatch (*not seeing Kenny*) Robinson Crusoe and his stupid friends are due for some bad luck.
Jack Boot How d'you know?
Blackpatch Just now I sees a great big albatross flying over the island.
Jack Boot Are albatrosses unlucky?
Kenny (*to the Audience*) They are if you stand underneath them!
Blackpatch Very unlucky—so now 'tis a good time to chat up the Cannibal Queen.
Jack Boot Aye, and what are we going to *give* the Cannibal Queen for showing us the treasure?
Kenny (*big reaction—aside to the Audience*) The treasure???
Blackpatch Simple, matey, we'll give her Robinson Crusoe's guns.
Kenny (*reacting with such panic that his voice is squeaky as he turns to the Audience*) Robinson Crusoe's guns???

Act II, Scene 2

Jack Boot But where does he keep them?
Blackpatch He rescued them from the shipwreck and he's stored them in the stockade.
Jack Boot (*evilly*) So we're going to creep into the stockade—
Blackpatch (*evilly*) Give the guns to the cannibals—
Jack Boot And that'll be that!
Blackpatch Yes... Robinson Crusoe? (*He puts his fingers across his throat and makes a gurgling noise*) Krrrrch!
Jack Boot Polly Perkins? (*Same business*) Krrrrch!
Blackpatch The Captain? (*Same business*) Krrrrch!
Jack Boot Mrs Crusoe? (*Same business*) Krrrrch!
Blackpatch } (*together, loudly*) And *Kenny* Crusoe? (*Same business and very*
Jack Boot } *loud gurgle*) Krrrrch!!!
Kenny (*hysterically gabbling*) Help! They're going to find the treasure, bribe the cannibals, attack the stockade, grab the guns, and kill us all off!!! (*In a suddenly slow, cultured and completely relaxed voice*) That was News at Ten, (*local place*). Goodnight. (*He nods his head solemnly*)

He exits unseen by the two Pirates

Blackpatch Here comes Wotta Woppa the Cannibal Queen.
Jack Boot We'll soon con her.

They both laugh wickedly

Wotta Woppa enters

Wotta Woppa Boola!
Blackpatch We wants you to help us, matey.
Wotta Woppa (*indignantly*) "Matey"? Me not matey, me Queenie.
Blackpatch We'll pay you good money, Queenie.
Wotta Woppa (*shaking her head furiously*) Boola dampo jampo.
Jack Boot Would you like *guns* better?
Wotta Woppa (*nodding her head eagerly*) Guns! Guns and boola dampo jampo! (*She makes gestures round her neck and at her ears*)
Blackpatch (*not understanding*) "Boola dampo jampo?"
Jack Boot She wants guns but she wants *jewellery* as well!
Blackpatch Jewellery? Leave this to me, matey, I've got an idea!

Blackpatch holds up a very large prop safety pin from inside his coat and at once the Queen is pleased

Wotta Woppa (*enthusiastically*) "Jewellery"?
Blackpatch Yes, very expensive jewellery. This is what in England we calls "a safety pin".
Wotta Woppa "Safety pin". (*She rolls her eyes in delight*) Safety pin. Yambi! Yambi!
Jack Boot There are only a few in the whole world. Very precious.
Wotta Woppa "Safety pin". (*She rolls her eyes some more*) Goody gum drops.
Blackpatch We knew you'd like it. We took it out of the nose of some singing cannibals many years ago.

Wotta Woppa What "singing cannibals"?
Blackpatch (*still very serious as he mentions a topical pop group*) Adam and the Ants, matey. (*He holds up the safety pin*) If we gives you this, will you take us to the Ruined Temple?
Wotta Woppa (*nodding*) Boola!
Blackpatch Robinson Crusoe and his friends must be defeated. They've become very truculent.
Wotta Woppa (*licking her lips expansively*) Goody goody, delicious!
Blackpatch I said truculent, not succulent.
Jack Boot And Robinson has built a *stockade*. Will you and your cannibals help us to attack the stockade?
Wotta Woppa (*nodding*) Boola!
Blackpatch Then here be the jewellery. (*He hands it over with great care as though it is of immense value*) There you are, Queenie, matey.

Blackpatch and Jack Boot exit sniggering together

Wotta Woppa (*proudly showing the pin to the Audience*) Safety pin! Me got safety pin! Isn't I a lucky gal? (*She waves the pin triumphantly*) See you later, alligator! In a while, crocodile! (*If the Audience has called out the "crocodile" bit, which they sometimes do, she looks with great pleasure at someone in the front rows*) You a cannibal? (*Much surprised, as though the person has replied*) You *is*?

Wotta Woppa exits

From the other side, the Captain enters, happily singing to himself. Friday follows him on

The Captain stops singing and is terrified when he notices Friday

Captain (*pointing to Friday*) Cannibal!
Friday (*looking behind him*) Where?
Captain You—cannibal.
Friday Me? Cannonball? BOOM? (*He mimes an explosion*)
Captain *Cannibal* not cannonball.
Friday (*shaking his head*) No understand.
Captain (*explaining*) If your father and your mother ate each other what would you be?
Friday An orphan.
Captain No, no. The natives—the people who don't play "follow my leader", they play "*swallow* my leader".
Friday Oh *cannibal!* (*Indignantly*) Me not cannibal. Oh dear me no, sir! Me *good* person! Me *Friday!* Call me Friday! Call me Friday!
Captain I will. What's your phone number?
Friday No, no. (*Impatiently*) Call me Friday! Call me Friday!
Captain (*doubtfully*) But you're a chocolate colour . . .
Friday (*giving up*) Then call me chocolate sundae.
Captain You're very brown.
Friday Don't just say brown say "Hovis".
Captain (*laughing*) You speak a bit of English!

Act II, Scene 2   51

Friday Well, *me* friend of Robinson Crusoe.
Captain You? A friend of Robinson's? Prove it!
Friday He comes from (*local place*).
Captain What are you talking about?
Friday Look, I didn't invent the name, mister, some potty Englishman did. He lives in . . . (*Saying the local name distinctly*)
Captain (*laughing*) And what do you know about (*local place*)?
Friday Not a lot! Except I hear they speak proper in (*local place*). *You* speak beautiful English. You teach me, because man, you speak just like—
Captain Roy Jenkins?
Friday No.
Captain Prince Charles?
Friday No.
Captain Who then?
Friday Spike Milligan.
Captain Gettartoffit!

The Captain chases Friday off and they both exit

Loud drum beats are heard and two Cannibals enter with a cut-out of a stewpot with firewood and red flames under it. Walking behind it—as though in it—are Mrs Crusoe and Kenny. Wotta Woppa accompanies them, looking delighted, together with other Cannibals

Mrs Crusoe } (*together, wailing*) No! Help us! Save me!
Kenny
Wotta Woppa (*singing, unaccompanied*) "Food, glorious food, specially when it's human." Oh yum yum, tum tum! (*She pats her stomach*) Dese two people is gonna be *delicious*—dey is gonna be finger lickin' good!
Mrs Crusoe I've heard of pot luck but this is ridiculous!
Kenny I'm always getting myself into hot water.
Wotta Woppa You wait till you come to da boil! Ha ha ha ha ha! (*To the Cannibals*) Dat gets a big laugh, don't it?
Cannibals (*agreeing and grinning*) Yah—oh yah!
Mrs Crusoe (*defiantly*) Now look here, you great big chocolate eclair.
Wotta Woppa (*angrily*) BOOLA! We cannibals have a motto—"If you can't beat 'em—EAT 'EM!" (*Shouting*) We want beans! We want beans!
Cannibals (*waving their spears*) We want beans! We want beans!
Kenny Baked beans or French Beans?
Wotta Woppa Human beans!
Kenny   } (*together, wailing*) No!
Mrs Crusoe
Wotta Woppa (*pointing to the pot*) Stewpot! Dis am *stewpot!* So what do you say about stewpot?
Kenny ("*Ed Stewpot*" *style*) Morneeng!
Wotta Woppa (*pleasantly; to Mrs Crusoe*) Ma dear, you make very nice soup.
Mrs Crusoe (*pleased*) Yes, I do. How did you know? I get a lot of stock and Oxo cubes and— (*She rubs her fingers together as in the Oxo commercial then realizes what's been said*) HELP! She means *I'll* make nice soup!

Kenny laughs smugly

Wotta Woppa (*to Kenny*) I like you. I dip you in da salt and eat you for ma tea!
Kenny (*not laughing*) She thinks I'm a stick of celery! (*To Wotta Woppa*) You—you—you animated Mars Bar!
Wotta Woppa (*furiously*) Boola!
Mrs Crusoe (*desperately*) We've got to escape—but how?
Kenny (*desperately*) I don't know!
Wotta Woppa When da water in da stewpot is boiling, we dance round da pot. And when we cannibals dance, *we dance*. Oh lordy, lordy, yes!
Mrs Crusoe (*catching on to this*) You *dance?* What do you dance?
Wotta Woppa We dance da tribal dance. Da medicine man invent it—it's called da Bupa! Good cannibal joke! (*Pointing to someone in the Audience*) If you don't get ma jokes, Ah have you for afters.
Mrs Crusoe A tribal dance? Oh, she doesn't want to dance that old thing does she, Kenny?
Kenny No, she wants to dance the *new* dance!
Wotta Woppa (*curiously*) New dance? What is da new dance?
Mrs Crusoe Oh everybody's doing it—it's called the (*local place*) One Step.
Wotta Woppa (*uncertainly*) Da (*local place*) One Step?
Kenny Yes! It's fabulous! You must have seen it on Top of the Flops.
Wotta Woppa Me interested in dances. You show me (*local place*) One Step.

Kenny and Mrs Crusoe step round from behind the pot

Mrs Crusoe (*to the Cannibals*) You'll enjoy this! Watch carefully!
Kenny Here we go!

Music starts. Best is a loud square dance or "The Valeta". Kenny and Mrs Crusoe do some mad dance steps and the Cannibals follow the steps with tremendous interest. Kenny and Mrs Crusoe now quickly teach them the steps with ad lib chatter. "You put your right foot out then move across there" (etc). The quick routine is such that one has to dance away to the left for part of it. When the Cannibals in their turn dance away to the left with their backs to Kenny and Mrs Crusoe our two friends grab this opportunity to leave

Kenny
Mrs Crusoe } (*together*) SCARPER!

They both run off quickly

The Cannibals continue to dance about and enjoy the dance then suddenly realize they have been duped. They, and the music, stop dead

Wotta Woppa
Cannibals } (*together, furiously*) BOOLA!

They wave their spears and chase after Mrs Crusoe and Kenny

Black-out

Scene 3

At Robinson Crusoe's Stockade

As Act II, Scene 1 with a six-foot-high stockade across the stage with a practical gate to it. (See scenery notes)

Drum beats are heard, then they fade. The Captain is urgently looking through a hole in the stockade fence

Captain (*wiping his mouth with his hand*) I'm thirsty!

Robinson Crusoe enters

Robinson I'm Robinson! I've just been checking all the guns but what's happening out there? (*He points beyond the stockade fence*)
Captain There's no-one out there, Robinson.
Robinson (*grimly*) They'll be here soon enough. Kenny heard the Pirates talking about Cannibals. Still, the stockade's nearly finished. All we want is some food to store in here.

Friday enters carrying a prop egg

Friday (*nodding his head*) Food!
Robinson A turtle's egg! Oh *good!*
Friday (*repeating the inflection*) Good!
Robinson (*pulling a face when he smells the egg*) *Not* so good.
Friday (*confused*) *Not* so good.
Robinson I should throw that egg away for good.
Friday (*more confused*) For good?
Robinson Yes, for good.
Friday But why is it for good?
Robinson Because it's bad.
Friday (*to the Audience; finger to forehead*) White man, boola, boola! (*He starts to exit then turns to the Audience*) Two mosquitoes were sitting on Robinson Crusoe—one said "I'm going now, but I'll meet you on Friday!" (*He laughs hilariously*) Ha ha ha—oh that's great, Friday, that's just great!

Friday exits, pleased with himself

Captain (*laughing*) I hope Friday's going to enjoy life when we all get back to London after our adventures!
Robinson Well, I've explained to him that it never stops raining and we British are mad.
Captain (*laughing*) How did you explain that?
Robinson I told him we sometimes black up our faces and do a show called the "Black and White Minstrels" so he said he'd put his face in a bucket of whitewash and join us.
Captain (*laughing*) Good answer!
Robinson I've been teaching him some of the songs they do.

Captain Man Friday in the Black and White Minstrel Show—that'd be a turn-up for the book!
Robinson (*laughing*) Right. (*He looks offstage*) Oh heavens, he's taken me at my word! You remember all the clothes we saved from the wreck? He's putting on a dinner jacket!

The introduction to Song 14 starts and Friday runs in. He still wears his desert island clothes but now has a dinner jacket over them, a black bow tie on elastic round his neck and white gloves

Friday gets down on one knee and sings in the Al Jolson style

Song 14

Robinson and the Captain join him for the short coda to this quick bit of "Minstrels" routine

After the song Friday exits. Loud cannibal drumbeats are heard and Bill and Ben run in, scared

Bill Cannibal war drums!
Ben What did the cannibal say when he saw the missionary asleep?
Bill I don't know. What did the cannibal say when he saw the missionary asleep?
Ben Look—breakfast in bed!
Robinson How can you two remain so calm when the cannibals are about to attack?
Ben Well, it's no good getting into a stew, is it?
Bill (*reciting*)   There was a young cannibal called Ned
              Who used to eat onions in bed.
Ben   His mother said "Sonny,
              That's not very funny,
              Why don't you eat people instead?"

Robinson laughs but the Captain is anxious

Captain This isn't the time for jokes. (*Calling*) Here everyone! And check that your guns are safe!
Robinson You're right! I know the Cannibals are still a long way off but we'd better be prepared. (*Calling*) Here everybody!

Friday, Polly and a couple of Sailors enter

The Captain points to each person as he delivers the warning

Captain Yes, be prepared or they'll eat you, and you, and you, and you, and you—(*he notices the parrot and crosses to it*)—they might even eat you!
Audience Busby!

Kenny enters

Kenny (*to the Audience*) Thanks, kids!

Everyone gathers in a group round Robinson as he now points to various places

Robinson You'd better be on guard there—and you, Captain, by the gate to

Act II, Scene 3   55

the stockade—you, Kenny, over there—you, Bill, and you, Ben, over there—Friday, there—and you, Polly, stay by me.

While Robinson is preparing for the attack three Cannibal heads appear over the stockade, followed by other Cannibal heads

The Audience will shout a warning

Robinson (*to the Audience*) Something wrong? It's what?
Audience Cannibals!
Kenny Meat balls! Delicious. I like them. I had some in a Wimpy and . . .
Ben Camphor balls? Can't hear!
Bill What cannonballs?
Polly We can't hear what you're saying!
Robinson (*realizing*) They mean CANNIBALS!

At this they all turn round and see the Cannibal heads. There is a dramatic chord as they react in panic. Everyone yells and rushes about the stage. Robinson and the Captain run up to the gate to secure it

Polly and a Sailor rush off to get the guns, which they return with immediately and hand round

Bill and Ben test the guns, Ben holding one the wrong way round and aiming at his foot

Bill Careful or you'll blow your big toe off!
Ben Sorry! (*Still being vague he now aims it at Bill's face*)
Bill Idiot! (*He pushes it away*)

Friday has a small plank ready to hit the enemy and Robinson holds a rifle. The Cannibal heads have disappeared. All wait anxiously

Robinson That's strange! Everything's gone quiet—what can you see, Captain?
Captain (*with a telescope at the hole in the fence*) I don't understand—they've all gone!
Polly It's a trick! I'm sure it's a trick!

They wait quietly. We hear Blackpatch's voice, desperate and sincere

Blackpatch (*off, behind the stockade; terrified*) Robinson Crusoe, help me! The Cannibals are coming back—please—help me to escape, matey!
Robinson No, Polly, it's not a trick. (*Calling*) Captain! Quick, before the Cannibals return! Open the gate for Blackpatch! He mustn't be eaten alive!
Captain Aye! Aye! Right Robinson! (*He opens the gate and stands aside*)

But now there are war cries! All the Cannibals charge in led by Wotta Woppa, Blackpatch and Jack Boot

There is dismay from our friends. Dramatic music, the fight is pitiful, for soon our friends are held at spear point—all in an upstage group

Cannibals Boola, Boola!
Wotta Woppa (*triumphantly pointing with her spear*) Omballi Booloo! Now you have had your chips! (*To her Cannibal followers*) Zoodoo?

Cannibals (*enthusiastically nodding agreement*) Zoodoo!
Blackpatch So, Robinson Crusoe, we meet again!
Jack Boot Only this time you'd better say your prayers! Ha ha ha!
Blackpatch (*to Polly*) Particularly you, my little lass. We're moving on to the Ruined Temple now, so we can dig up the treasure. Only we're not going *alone*, are we, Jack Boot?
Jack Boot No, shipmate, not us.
Blackpatch We need a little female company—and you're the little female.
Polly No!

Blackpatch grabs Polly, and holds up his pistol

Blackpatch (*threatening everyone*) Let one of 'eee step forward and I'll blow you to smithereens, as sure as my name's Bartholomew Blackpatch. If any of you move I'll make mincemeat out of you.
Wotta Woppa (*big round eyes rolling at this thought*) Mincemeat! Good idea!

Blackpatch pulls the struggling Polly from the group who are powerless to help her because of the Cannibal spears

Blackpatch Come on, Jack Boot! We'll soon reach the treasure, shiver me timbers, wet me whistle and stap me vitals! Ha ha ha!
Jack Boot (*echoing the laugh*) Ho ho ho!
Blackpatch (*leering at Polly*) This way, Polly Perkins, matey.

Blackpatch, Jack Boot and Polly exit through the gate

Wotta Woppa And now foolish people, your time has come! Oh lordy, lordy, yes!

The Cannibals become a sort of tableau and in front is Wotta Woppa waving her spear menacingly

Dere is two kinds of black people on dis island. Da good ones like Man Friday dere. And da bad ones like me heyah. Ain't dat right, Cannibals?
Cannibals Boola!
Wotta Woppa (*to Robinson and his friends*) So you is all going to *die!*
Kenny (*to the Audience*) There's one person that could help us—but that person is thousands of miles away!

There is a fanfare. Mrs Crusoe enters* through the stockade gate, wearing a blonde wig, royal blue suit and an enormous blue rosette on her label

Mrs Crusoe (*very slowly*) I ... man ... aged ... to ... get ... away ... from ... Down ... ing ... Street.
Wotta Woppa (*aggressively defiant*) And just who is you?
Mrs Crusoe (*very graciously*) I ... am ... Mar ... garet ... That ... cher ...

At this, Wotta Woppa and the Cannibals scream the place down and exit at the double through the gate

* Note: *The character adopted by Mrs Crusoe for her entrance can be any topical political or television figure as long as she clearly announces who she is and thus gains instant recognition by the Audience. There may even be a local personality you could choose!*

Act II, Scene 4

There is general rejoicing at their departure

Black-out

Scene 4

In the Forest of Grunting Gorillas
Tabs or a frontcloth of dense tropical jungle with creepers and bright flowers
Jack Boot enters, followed by Blackpatch dragging on the struggling Polly

Blackpatch Come on, my little matey!
Polly Let me go! You'll pay for this when Robinson finds you!
Jack Boot When Robinson Crusoe finds *me*, may I have the pleasure of putting my sword through him? (*He lunges fiercely as though holding his sword*)
Blackpatch He's all yours, matey—but he'll never escape from them Cannibals.
Polly (*scared*) What d'you mean?
Blackpatch (*gloating*) At this 'ere very moment they're poking their spears into Robinson's human flesh, *wondering what it's going to taste like!* Ha ha ha!
Jack Boot (*echoing him*) Ho ho ho!

Jack Boot's laughter causes him to turn away so that he is looking offstage, away from where they entered

(*Excitedly*) Shipmate—there it is! (*He points to the wings*)
Blackpatch (*excitedly*) AT LAST! The Ruined Temple—the Temple of the Snake! (*To Polly; menacingly*) Little matey, I've been told all about that there snake. 'Tis sacred to the Cannibals—they be terrified of it—and so will you be!
Polly You're vile and you're horrible!
Blackpatch Oh, I hope I am, little matey. We *must* live up to the legend of "Blackpatch, the Wicked Pirate", mustn't we?
Jack Boot This way, Blackpatch—and stop flirting!
Blackpatch (*laughing*) "Stop flirting"—oh, that's very rich, that is! Come on, Miss Polly Perkins of Paddington Green!

As she is dragged off, Polly turns her head back, calling

Polly Robinson! Help me, Robinson!
Blackpatch I don't suppose 'ee can 'ear you, little matey! Because right now he's being *fattened up for a Cannibal supper*. On the menu it says "Roasted Robinson"! Ha ha ha!

Jack Boot exits and Blackpatch follows, dragging Polly with him

The other side the Captain and Mrs Crusoe enter. She has changed her appearance back to being Mrs Crusoe and wears her former dame wig and has put a bright coat over her last costume and carries a big handbag

Mrs Crusoe (*highpitched rendering*) "A sleepy lagoon, a tropical moon, and you on an island ..."
Captain Oh, Mrs Crusoe, the way you defeated the Cannibals! I was dead scared until you arrived—all that worry's given me a terrible headache.
Mrs Crusoe Well, you won't find any aspirins in the jungle.
Captain Why not?
Mrs Crusoe The parrots ... eat ... 'em ... all. (*Triumphantly to the Audience*) Get it? The parrots ... eat ... 'em ... all—paracetamol! Good isn't it! (*She sees they aren't with her*) Please yerself.
Captain When I see someone like you standing up to the Cannibals I begin to understand what Women's Lib is all about.
Mrs Crusoe Oh women can do far better than men! (*To the Audience*) Can't we, girls? We women are on the attack now!
Captain (*proud of her*) Yes, women like you are revolting.
Mrs Crusoe You cheeky monkey! Women like me are revolting? I've never been so insulated in my life! What a thing to say! (*Irritated, she walks to Busby's corner*)
Audience Busby!

Kenny runs on, shouting his thanks, followed by Bill, Ben and Robinson, who is holding the chart

Robinson (*studying the chart*) We passed the Cannibal village, then we went North. That's it—here we are!
All Where?
Robinson (*dramatically*) In the Forest of Grunting Gorillas!!
Kenny (*laughing*) The Forest of Grunting Gorillas? Whoever heard of grunting gorillas?

They all laugh but we hear loud "Ug-ug" grunts off

Bill (*terrified*) I did! I heard a grunting gorilla just then!

Everyone laughs at him but more "Ug-ugs" are heard

Robinson Bill's right—I heard it as well!
Ben But how will we know if the gorilla comes?
Kenny (*to the Audience*) You'll shout out and tell us, won't you?
Audience Yes!
Mrs Crusoe Then we'd better have a rehearsal—I'll pretend to be the gorilla.
Kenny That won't be difficult.
Mrs Crusoe (*hitting Kenny with her handbag*) Quiet, Kenny. (*To the Audience*) I'll go off like this and then I'll creep back like a gorilla.
All All right—you do that, Mum—let's see what happens (*etc*)

Mrs Crusoe exits and enters at once lumbering about and scratching like a gorilla

The others encourage the Audience to shout

Audience Gorilla!
Mrs Crusoe (*to the Audience*) You need to be a bit louder because we don't want to be grabbed by a gorilla—I'll do it again.

Act II, Scene 4

Mrs Crusoe exits and enters as before

Audience Gorilla!
Robinson Mum, that was great!
Bill Good idea that!
Ben Well done, Mrs Crusoe!
Kenny Once more, Mum!
Mrs Crusoe All right, dear!

Mrs Crusoe exits, then enters again. But this time the Gorilla follows her on, unseen by those on stage

Audience Gorilla!
Robinson (*cheerfully, to the Audience*) Yes, that's it!
Kenny (*to the Audience*) Well done, folks—thanks for your help!
Bill }
Ben } (*together; to the Audience*) Super! Smashing!

They chat away to the Audience but the Audience will repeatedly call out the warning

Audience Gorilla!
All (*to the Audience*) What?
Kenny You mean, you saw a gorilla?
Audience Yes!

The Gorilla exits

Bill But where?
Audience There!

Everyone looks to where the Gorilla has gone

Mrs Crusoe Nothing there now, is there? Now don't be potty—you called out "Gorilla" when there's nothing there!

The Gorilla comes bounding on, scratching and grunting

Audience Gorilla!

Our five friends again miss seeing the Gorilla, tell the Audience that they're imagining it, then stand in a line chatting about the fact that gorillas don't live in forests, besides they're only found in Africa (etc, etc)

During this, the Gorilla enters, taps Bill on the shoulder, he sees the Gorilla, screams and exits. Then the Gorilla taps in turn Robinson, Kenny and Ben, all of whom first pull a face of comedy terror, and then exit yelling

Now Mrs Crusoe is alone at CS, *the Gorilla being at the side of the stage, scratching and making its Ug-ug noises*

Mrs Crusoe (*opening her handbag; chatting to the Audience*) Oh, I am hungry. Well, you do get hungry on a desert island you know—that's why I picked this off a palm tree when I was passing. (*She takes a banana out of her handbag and starts to peel it, ignoring the Audience's shouts*) I mean, I knew we'd got a long walk to the Ruined Temple so I thought a bit of food would be nice.

Mrs Crusoe is about to bite at the banana but turns to the Audience instead, as they are shouting to her

What's the matter? What? I can't hear you!

Mrs Crusoe turns away from the banana that she is holding out and talks to the Audience. The Gorilla bounds across, grabs the banana, and then stands behind her, and "eats" it

(*Cheerfully, to the Audience*) I'm sorry, dears, but I can't hear a blooming word you're saying, so back we go to eating the ban— (*She goes to eat it but it isn't there*) Who's nicked my nana?

Audience Gorilla!

Mrs Crusoe (*laughing*) Don't be dotty! There isn't a gor— (*She at last sees it*) Oh blimey! It's Chewbacca from *Star Wars*! (*To the Audience*) He's a gorilla and I'm a gonner! How can I escape? What'll I do? (*A big idea dawns on her*) I know!

Mrs Crusoe opens her handbag, takes out a hand mirror and gives it to the Gorilla who has been grunting a great deal and jumping up and down with heavy thuds. It gazes into the mirror, the music plays "A Pretty Girl is Like a Melody" and pats its head, smooths its hair and strokes its eyebrows

The Gorilla exits, engrossed in its own reflection

Mrs Crusoe (*shouting happily, with great relief*) SAVED!

She runs off the other side to a few bars of vaudeville music

Black-out

Scene 5

The Ruined Temple of the Sacred Snake

Palm Tree wings, backcloth of a jungle and ruined temple. In front of it is a cut-out of a crumbling statue of a primitive god, Siamese style, its imposing base or plinth containing the treasure which at the moment is hidden. (See scenery notes)

The Cannibals and Wotta Woppa (who is proudly holding her big safety pin like a sceptre) are singing and dancing

Song 15

During the routine, the Queen ushers in the girl dancer who is dressed as a snake and all watch the Snake Dance solo (Music 15(a))

PRODUCTION ROUTINE

Wotta Woppa (*after the routine; calling off*) Boola!

With her safety pin, Wotta Woppa waves on Blackpatch, who is holding the struggling Polly, and Jack Boot

Act II, Scene 5   61

Blackpatch Well, your majesty matey, fair's fair. I gave you that beautiful safety pin so you give me the beautiful treasure.
Wotta Woppa (*shaking her head*) Oh, no, no, no, man! Me do not know where da treasure is.
Jack Boot You know all right. You can't fool Captain Blackpatch and me, your majesty matey!
Blackpatch (*threatening her*) You can't con a callous and crafty cut-throat whose charismatic career is covered in cruelty and cunning, now can you, Queenie?
Wotta Woppa (*scared*) Me not sure Mr Blackpatch, but me think it is among da rocks dere! (*She points off*)
Jack Boot (*looking off*) Among the rocks, eh? The Treasure of Tobago!
Blackpatch The Treasure of Tobago—delicious! (*To Polly*) Come on, little matey, don't you want a gold necklace round that pretty little neck of yours?
Polly No—I want a rope round that great big ugly unwashed neck of *yours!*
Blackpatch You're like a wild tiger, just how I like my women!
Polly Oh, what is to become of me?
Blackpatch You're to become Mrs Blackpatch, the toast of Tobago! (*To the Audience*) Sounds better than *Mrs Robinson Crusoe* doesn't it?
Audience No!
Blackpatch Ach shurrup! (*Calling to all*) Come on, you land-lubbers! And you, your majesty, matey! (*Sneering at his crony*) And you, Jack Boot, waiting for your booty are you? I wouldn't trust you as far as I could throw you! (*To all*) Come on.

Blackpatch grabs Polly, and Wotta Woppa signals to the muttering Cannibals to follow

Wotta Woppa Boola! Yussambo!
Jack Boot (*to Wotta Woppa, scared of Blackpatch now*) I don't know what to make of Captain Blackpatch.
Wotta Woppa How about a great big casserole?

Everyone exits except Jack Boot

As Jack Boot is about to go he trips up, apparently hurting his ankle. He reaches down to stroke his ankle, his back to CS

Man Friday enters, carrying a tube and a kitchen bowl

Friday (*to the Audience*) Jack Boot is naughty man. I follow him all through jungle. (*He holds up the tube*) Here is a blow pipe with a dart in it—and here is a bowl of British Rail porridge!

Friday quickly puts the bowl on the ground, dips the blow pipe in the bowl, holds it to his mouth and makes a loud puffing and blowing noise as though actually blowing. We hear a swanee whistle effect and suddenly Jack Boot jerks himself upright, lets out a great cry and puts his hand to where the dart has supposedly entered his seat

Jack Boot then staggers off. There is a loud crash offstage

I got him in the end! Good riddance to bad rubbish! (*He bows to the Audience*) Thank you very much.

Friday exits gleefully with bowl and tube

There is dramatic tingling music and Robinson enters, his sword in his belt, holding the chart and pacing out the steps

Robinson Thirty-one . . . thirty-two . . . thirty-three . . . thirty-four . . .

Blackpatch enters. He drags the struggling Polly with him

Polly Let go of me. Robinson!
Robinson Polly! And *you*, Blackpatch. (*He quickly tucks the chart into his belt*)
Blackpatch Yes, matey, it's Captain Blackpatch, and this is going to be our last meeting. (*He draws his sword*)
Robinson (*drawing his sword*) Yes—because after it you'll be dead!
Blackpatch No, matey, you will.
Polly Robinson, be careful!
Robinson Don't worry, Polly. (*To Blackpatch*) Big head!

Duel/excitement music starts, and the antagonists circle each other shouting out insults

Blackpatch (*furiously*) What did you say? (*Swiping at the air with his sword*) My sword is as clean as a whistle.
Robinson A clean sword for a dirty fighter!
Blackpatch You know what happens to lads like you wot fights pirates like me?
Robinson Yes, this! (*He flips his sword at Blackpatch and gooses him*)
Blackpatch Ow! That hurt!
Robinson You bloodthirsty buccaneer!
Blackpatch I hates you, Robinson Crusoe, and we'll fight to the death!
Robinson To the death and the death will be yours!

Blackpatch and Robinson fight, watched by the anxious Polly. Soon Robinson's sword slides under Blackpatch's upstage arm and Blackpatch lets out a cry and starts to exit, dying melodramatically. As he exits, his magic book falls on to the ground from his belt. With a final desperate cry, he staggers to the wings and falls to the ground

Blackpatch crawls off

Robinson VICTORY!

Polly and Robinson run to each other and embrace

Polly (*happily*) Oh, Robinson! I must go and tell the others Blackpatch is dead!
Robinson All right—you go and tell them the great news and I'll try and find the treasure!

Polly exits

Act II, Scene 5

(*Taking out the chart*) Now I'm in the Ruined Temple, so what next? (*Reading*) "The treasure lies forty paces due East!" (*He returns to where he stood before Blackpatch entered*) This was thirty-five so on to thirty-six... thirty-seven... thirty-eight... thirty-nine... forty. (*He is now at the base of the statue*)

Kenny, Bill and Ben, Mrs Crusoe, Man Friday, Polly and Captain Perkins enter. (Due to a later quick change, sometimes Man Friday doesn't enter here)

Mrs Crusoe (*seeing the idol*) Oh look—it's Cyril Smith in the jungle!
Kenny How are you getting on, Robinson?
Robinson Well, I've got this far but now the treasure chart says I must consult the magic book—but *what* magic book?
Kenny (*looking round*) Where's Paul Daniels?
Polly (*remembering*) I read out from a magic book that belonged to Blackpatch.
Robinson What's this? (*He picks up the book dropped by Blackpatch*)
Polly That's it!
Mrs Crusoe (*sentimentally*) What a shame you killed that lovely big man, Robinson. He was evil and twisted and cruel and kinky—just how I like my men!
Ben Naughty girl!
Robinson Never mind that, mother! Let's look up "Treasure" in the book.

They all gather round Mrs Crusoe

Mrs Crusoe (*turning the pages*) T for Treasure... T for Treasure... oh, here it is. (*Loudly*) "The secret of the treasure of Tobago lies in one magic word and that one word is Jack—" (*Horrified*) The page is ripped! That's all there is! Just the word "Jack"!
Robinson Then we need a magic word beginning with "Jack".
Kenny Jack Knife—Jack daw...
Mrs Crusoe Glenda Jackson.
Bill Jacko—
Ben Jackee—Jackee—
Polly Jackay—Jackeye—

They appeal to the Audience who will soon call out "Jackanory"

Friday Jackeye... Jackeye... er... er...
Mrs Crusoe Jacka... Jacka... Jacka... any ideas?
Audience Jackanory!
Mrs Crusoe What?
Kenny Can't hear!
Audience Jackanory!
Robinson JACKANORY! That may be it! (*To the Audience*) Thanks! Come on, all of you, let's shout it out together.

All on stage (and the Audience) shout "JACKANORY"

Robinson Nothing happened. Once again—and much louder this time!

All shout again. The Lights flicker, there is a great thunder sound, a loud fanfare and all the cast look at the stone statue which reveals its treasure (see scenery notes). Everyone rushes up and collects various glittering items

Mrs Crusoe (*excitedly, to Kenny*) I'm with the gold and the silver and the jewels and the diamonds—what are you with?
Kenny I'm with the Woolwich!
Bill All this money! What shall we do with it?
Ben (*singing*) "Come and talk, talk, talk to the Midland, the listening bank." (*He does the gallumping walk as in the commercial*)
Kenny Yes, very good money. But how do we spend it?
Polly Oh, that's right. (*To the others*) How do we get back to England?
Mrs Crusoe I know! (*She holds up the magic book*) S for Ship! Just a minute ... (*turning pages*) S for Ship ... S for Ship ... Aha! (*She reads the spell like a chant*) Abracadabra, Abracadee, We call upon the Spirit of Light—presto deliria ... mumbo jumbo ... hocus pocus ... mumbo jumbo ... hocus pocus ...

As she chants, "Rule Britannia" is played softly

The music builds as two sailors enter and salute. Between them Lord Nelson (with the traditional one arm, eye shade and cocked hat) enters

Kenny (*pointing*) Trafalgar Square is down there and first right.

All laugh including Nelson

Mrs Crusoe (*waving the book*) I knew it would work!
Nelson (*to Robinson*) I'm delighted to meet you, Mr er ...
Bill (*stepping forward, cheekily*) Barnacle Bill. Can I have your autograph? How's Lady Hamilton?
All Quiet!
Robinson I'm Robinson Crusoe, sir, but how come you're *here?*
Nelson We came ashore to collect fresh water—saw your stockade—followed your tracks—and we'll be delighted to take you home!
All Fabulous—great—thanks!
Nelson (*declaiming*) England expects every man this day will do his duty!
Robinson And will take us home to England—Home and Beauty!

There is a fanfare as Nelson and Robinson shake hands

Everyone cheers and exits

Wotta Woppa enters from the other side, looks across the stage and gasps. (Note: this scene between Wotta Woppa and Blackpatch can be played in front of tabs to allow longer for the scene change to the Finale set)

Wotta Woppa (*to the Audience, amazed*) Dat wicked pirate, Captain Blackpatch—Ah thought he was dead as a dodo but he ain't—he alive! Look!

Blackpatch enters

Act II, Scene 6   65

Boola! Ah saw Robinson Crusoe put his bread knife through you! So how come you is alive? How is you saved?
Blackpatch (*holding up a big bottle*) Phyllosan fortifies the over forties.
Wotta Woppa (*amazed*) Dat little bottle save you? Well shut ma mouth.
Blackpatch Aye, it gave me strength so that I could return to you, my exotic little beauty. (*Flirting heavily*) Come and have a date behind the palms.
Wotta Woppa (*to the Audience*) He's evil and he's twisted, but lordy, lordy, he is sexy! (*To Blackpatch*) What you want from me, you wicked man?
Blackpatch I likes plump girls. I'd like you to come back to England with me, your majesty matey.
Wotta Woppa Ah don't think so. "Yesterday in Parliament" and dat Tony Blackburn on da radio every day? No thank you.
Blackpatch (*enticingly*) I'd buy us a home in (*local snob area*)
Wotta Woppa Mmmm . . . (*She repeats the address*) Dat's very tempting but Ah don't think so.
Blackpatch Why not?
Wotta Woppa Ah'll tell you, honey. (*She sings in an extrovert Sophie Tucker Red Hot Momma style*)

Song 16

After the song and dance, Blackpatch and Wotta Woppa exit

CURTAIN

SCENE 6

On the Way Home

Either one of the ship frontcloths or in front of the tabs

Man Friday enters, dressed in a mortar board and gown and a pin-stripe suit. Halfway across the stage he stops

Friday (*speaking very distinctly and ultra-perfectly*) Hullo. I would like to stop and have a chat but I'm rather busy—you see, I start next term as the new English Master at (*local college or school*)! (*He starts to exit but notices Busby in the corner, and goes towards the cage*)
Audience Busby!

Kenny runs on and Friday exits

Kenny Thanks, kids! And thanks for looking after Busby all through the performance. It's time to say hullo to him! (*He collects the cage and talks to the "bird"*) Who's a lovely feller then? (*He reacts greatly as he looks in the cage*) Blimey, it isn't a feller—it's a bird! What I mean is, it's a female! I know it's a female 'cos it's laid some eggs! Now you've been smashing looking after Busby for me, so who wants a chocolate egg?

The Audience calls out, Kenny takes out some small chocolate eggs that have been in the bottom of the cage since the start of the pantomime. With ad libs he throws out the eggs to the Audience

Mrs Crusoe enters, having changed her costume

Mrs Crusoe Kenny, what's all the noise about?
Kenny We've discovered Busby's a she, not a he!
Mrs Crusoe (*laughing*) I'm like that only the other way round! No, the real reason I've come to see you is this. I want you to help me think up a last song for us all to sing.
Kenny Something to do with Robinson Crusoe?
Mrs Crusoe Yes. Something to do with galleons and ships and sailing the sea—got any ideas?

Note: You will find that the Audience will call out the title!

Kenny (*ignoring the Audience*) Er . . . Something to do with ships and sailing the sea?
Mrs Crusoe Yes. (*To the Audience*) Unless you've got some ideas? ("*Hearing*" *the Audience*) What a marvellous idea!
Kenny Perfect idea! So let's each have a team to sing with. Let's cut the Audience in two—it won't hurt much—this is my side!
Mrs Crusoe And this is my side, so prepare yourselves for singing—everybody cough. (*When the Audience is ready*) Now join Mrs Croaky Crusoe and off we go! (*She conducts her half of the Audience in the short song*)

Song 17

Kenny (*after this chorus*) That's no good!
Mrs Crusoe What's wrong with it, you rude boy? (*To her side of the Audience*) It was beautiful, wasn't it?
Audience Yes!—No! (*etc*)
Kenny But it needs some movement! They can't just sit there like stuffed owls when they sing.
Mrs Crusoe You're quite right, dear. (*To the Audience*) We need some movement. So get out your scarves! Get out your hankies! Get out your pension books!
Kenny Hold up your coats! Come on! That's it! Lovely! Hold them above your heads—that's it. Now sway in time! Sway—sway! (*He conducts the swaying of arms*)
Mrs Crusoe Be like a crowd of football supporters—only don't rip up the seats for pete's sake.

Mrs Crusoe and Kenny join forces and all sing the Songsheet. After the Songsheet, they both call out and wave to the Audience

Mrs Crusoe Bye now!
Kenny We've got to go or we'll be late!
Mrs Crusoe Yes, we mustn't be late for Robinson's wedding! See you later!

Mrs Crusoe and Kenny exit

Act II, Scene 7

The last eight bars of "Rule Britannia" are loudly played to continue the nautical theme and then one of the up tempo songs in the pantomime is used so that the Audience will clap in time to the Finale Walk Down music

Song 4 (reprise)

The tabs open on to:

Scene 7

The Nautical Wedding of Robinson Crusoe

Either a backcloth of a huge Union Jack, or the same as Act One, Scene One, but with bunting and Union Jacks everywhere—see scenery notes. If possible Mrs Crusoe can enter in a dress made of Union Jacks, and the Juveniles wave small Union Jacks

All enter as arranged for

Finale Walk Down

Then Blackpatch holds up his hand and begins the finale couplets

Blackpatch	Well, mateys, here's the Finale rhyme!
Polly	Because it's the end of the pantomime!
Queen	Ah apologize, Ah sorry 'Cos Ah've been very wicked!
Friday	I'm going back to Tobago To see the West Indies play cricket!
Bill	We hate to say goodbye
Ben	But now it's time to do so!
Kenny	We hope you liked the pantomime Ta! Ta! From Kenny Crusoe!
Mrs Crusoe	If I say, have you enjoyed yourselves You'd better answer yes!
Robinson	So goodbye from Robinson Crusoe— And of course God bless!

All reprise the main up tempo song—probably Song 2

Finale Curtain

Note: If in your production the Cannibals wear costumes and make-up that cannot be changed in time for the Finale, then we can make use of this fact. Substitute the above couplets for this arrangement. After the walk down, Mrs Crusoe steps forward and says:

Mrs Crusoe	We hope that you enjoyed the show Just one more word before we go—

All, and particularly the Cannibals who wave their spears at this, shout out:
All BOOLA!!!
All reprise the main up tempo song—probably Song 2

Finale Curtain

SCENERY, COSTUME, AND PRODUCTION SUGGESTIONS

SCENERY

This pantomime has been presented professionally in large theatres with a considerable amount of scenery, and you, too, may wish for a spectacular production. But in a recent amateur production the Ship was a permanent set for all Act I, and palm tree wings plus upstage cyclorama were used for Act II. This economy works well for a medium or small stage.

ACT I

Scene 1 (London Docks) has simple wings of a dockland pub one side and warehouses the other. Upstage centre is the Ship. There is a rostrum upstage and in front of it are two cut-outs representing the bulwarks. Between these two cut-outs is a gap of about four feet, at the centre of which is a slope down stage, for the gangway. The mast is a cut-out at upstage centre, behind or on the rostrum, and on each side of it are practical sails. Behind the mast, hiding some of the cyclorama is a cut-out of the stern with big galleon-style lanterns. You may like to add a ship's wheel, and some "ship's railing" balustrades. **Scene 2** (The Poop Deck) is tabs or a frontcloth. **Scene 3** (The Galley) is the Ship without the gangway, the wings being rigging and blue sky. Set in front of the Ship is a very simple inset galley scene consisting of flats or cut-outs representing the back wall of the galley. At SR is the other wall made of flats or cut-outs, with a practical porthole, merely a hole in the scenery. Paint this galley in bright colours as it is entirely a comedy scene—there are no scenery requirements for the comedy except a large kitchen table, domestic props and the simple porthole, through which things are thrown into the wings. You may need a stage cloth on the floor. **Scene 4** (Poop Deck again) is either tabs, in which case the signalling light will flicker on and off from the wings, or a frontcloth of the Ship's prow with deck boards in perspective, with the rest of the cloth representing the sea with the horizon almost half way up the cloth. (The Audience is looking at a ship sailing directly away from them, in perspective.) On the horizon, fix a pea light and, when the stage is dimly lit, this works fine as the signalling light. Or you may wish to open the tabs for about six feet and show a flat of bulwarks and the sea with horizon painted on, the pea light in position in the manner already explained. **Scene 5** (Main Deck) is rigging and blue sky for the wings, with the Ship UC. The cut-outs representing the bulwarks have been pushed together, the mast is now downstage of them (for The Strange Shipwreck, see production notes). **Scene 6** (Demon Oylslick's Gruesome Grotto) is tabs or a frontcloth of dark and unattractive seaweed and rocks. If thin, blue, horizontal lines are painted over these rocks, etc, this suggests that we are under the sea. **Scene 7** (The Ship now under the sea) is the shipwrecked galleon as it was at the end of

Scene 5, but in front of it are cut-outs of bright and attractive pink coral, plus light green and blue shells of various shapes and coloured rocks and seaweed plants growing upwards. Centre stage is a large (say eight feet high) fan-shaped shell that hides most of the mast and creates our Transformation Scene atmosphere. Sequins and glitter dust should be liberally applied to these cut-outs. Sometimes a coral and seaweed cut-out cloth is flown in, it being in front of the Ship which is seen through the big arched opening in this cloth. A ripple machine to represent the effect of water can be inexpensively hired from disco prop shops, or from Theatre Projects Ltd, 10 Long Acre, London WC2.

ACT II
This act has palm tree wings throughout.
Scene 1 (The Island) has a cyclorama to represent the sea and seashore and upstage is a cut-out of rocks and ferns. Rising from it are several four feet high sticks with skulls and shrunken heads on them plus tattered black ribbons hanging from beneath the skulls in the voodoo/cannibal style. Among them is a cut-out of a tall thin rock or broken palm tree trunk or African-looking totem pole that Man Friday will be tied to. **Scene 2** (Cannibal Village and Stewpot) is tabs or a frontcloth of wooden huts in a jungle clearing and the stewpot itself is a cut-out that is brought on stage by the cannibals (see production notes). **Scene 3** (The Stockade) is the same as Scene 1 but with a simple stockade fence that is about seven feet high right across the stage and about two thirds upstage. It's a cut-out painted to look as if it's made of upright stakes tied together with thongs—see illustrated books of Robinson Crusoe. At its centre is a practical gate in the stockade, the same height as the stockade fence. The gate should open onto the stage. **Scene 4** (Forest of Grunting Gorillas) is tabs or a frontcloth of a tropical forest with much tangled undergrowth and bright flowering creepers. **Scene 5** (Ruined Temple) is an upstage cut-out of jungle plants and huge ferns, or a dropcloth of the same that hides the cyclorama. In front of this is a cut-out of a weird, creeper-covered stone temple, with a ruined Buddha-like statue with big plinth or base that in fact contains the treasure—see production notes. The jungle, temple and statue can be all one cut-out if a small stage is used— only the statue's base need be practical. **Scene 6** is the Songsheet in front of tabs or a frontcloth. **Scene 7** is the Nautical Wedding which is a Patriotic Finale in the Victorian pantomime style. Either the backcloth is an entire Union Jack with Union Jacks now over the palm tree wings, or we return to the main deck of the ship and hang large Union Jacks where the sails were. Use the gangway at centre stage again for the Finale walk down, and use bunting for rigging.

COSTUME SUGGESTIONS
Robinson wears a principal boy's blue naval style uniform and opens Act II with a pantomime version of the legendary "Desert Island" costume. **Polly** usually wears a blue dress in Act I and a torn, shipwrecked version of this in Act II. **Mrs Crusoe** wears outrageous Dame costumes, maybe a bit "naval" as she is the ship's cook. She wears a floppy mob cap or chef's hat for the Galley

scene but if it is made of plastic this fact must be hidden from the audience or the moment when water is poured down on to her (which gets an excellent laugh) won't get any laugh at all because there is no discomfort for her. She wears a Wren costume for the mop drill scene. Her desert island costume is comically Hawaiian or is a tattered dress covered in seaweed with a bra of two prop shells or even two saucepan lids over a pink T shirt. As the Finale is Patriotic it is right if her Finale Costume is made of Union Jacks, or let her carry as an open parasol a Union Jack umbrella with smaller Union Jacks round it like a crazy sort of fringe.

Kenny Crusoe wears a comedy sailor's uniform, as do the Bosun and Mate. Maybe Kenny's is red and theirs are blue, and they wear horizontally striped jerseys—the costumes in H.M.S. *Pinafore* are a good guide. The **Captain** has a three-cornered hat and pantomime version of a blue eighteenth-century coat with white cravat, like Captain Bligh. **Blackpatch** wears a darkly sinister pirate's costume and you may find he needs a brightly coloured ostrich feather in his huge hat—sometimes he is dressed almost as Charles II. The black eye patch needs a hole piercing in it so that he can see easily—the audience doesn't notice this. **Jack Boot** is the traditional pirate and it's a great help to browse through pirate books in the public library. **Old Jim** wears a long coat and probably has a white wig and beard and he hobbles with a crutch under the arm, or with a walking stick.

Man Friday and **Queen Wotta Woppa** can wear black jersey over their bodies but you may prefer them to wear body make-up. The Queen is usually played by a plump person with a great sense of humour and she wears a grass skirt and black top or a tropically exotic bodice and some feathered headdress on her fuzzy-wuzzy wig, and maybe war paint on her face and plenty of beads and bracelets clanking about. **Lord Nelson** is exactly as pictures portray him—one arm, the eye patch, hat and knee breeches. He can be a sort of "second principal boy" if this is needed.

Demon Oylslick is best wearing black with a headdress like a black drum and with plenty of strips of black plastic hanging down to the ground. He has long black fringe hanging from his sleeves and a ghoulish black and white face. Black tights are better than black trousers under the fringed gown effect. His black gloves have exaggeratedly long fingers as he does a good deal of smarmy gesturing. **Fairy Detergenta** wears a very bright white and pretty costume in keeping with her name and as the necessary contrast to Demon Oylslick. Except for Robinson and Mrs Crusoe, the principals can wear the same costumes throughout.

CHORUS COSTUMES
The **Sailors** are probably mainly female and their costumes are in H.M.S. *Pinafore* style. As Pirates, *everyone* wears a black eye patch and as the Pirates are in fact mainly females, prop beards and moustaches are useful and funny. Three-cornered hats, headscarves with gold earrings sewn on, and prop daggers held in the teeth—the effect should be a strip cartoon version of bloodthirsty and wildly extrovert pirates, regardless of what sex is playing these villains. The costumes are such that Bill and Ben can re-enter after the comedy drill routine and thus swell the pirate horde if you wish, and the

audience doesn't recognize them. You will find that from the waist downwards, the pirates can wear the same costume as when sailors—it's the heads and faces that need the costume change.

Demon Oylslick's **Minions** are usually Juveniles and if so, they wear similar costumes to Oylslick and black make-up or black domino masks—they are not attractive juveniles in this scene, they are like their master and are horrible. If adults play the Minions, the same notes apply. Wide black plastic strips hanging down over the costumes do suggest oil very well. The **Sea Fairy People** wear light blue and sea green, a variation on fairyland costumes, the men are sometimes stern **Guards**, in King Neptune style, with sea green "ponchos" over their sailor costumes.

The **Cannibals** wear afro wigs, black jersey to neck and wrists, black tights and gloves. Both sexes wear grass skirts and feathers in their wigs and black faces or masks—a useful idea is half masks so that the mouth is free for dialogue, only the jaw and neck needing to be made-up black. Sometimes there isn't time to remove this black make-up and there is an alternative finale couplet in case this situation occurs. You may like two of the Chorus to remain as friendly sailors throughout, in which case they enter as attendant sailors to Lord Nelson at his arrival, and earlier are part of the friendly ship's crew. **Finale costumes** are Sailor, and some carry Union Jacks on poles, or as mentioned, you may find that the Chorus can be in Cannibal costumes for the whole of Act II.

PRODUCTION SUGGESTIONS

The three **lanterns** required in the comedy Galley scene are either arranged so that when quickly lowered they don't quite hit the people's heads, or are made of something harmless and lightweight.

The Pirate Fight. This needs excitement music in the silent film piano accompaniment style, perhaps Greig's "Hall of the Mountain King" and each hit from an assailant needs emphasizing with percussion crashes. Far the best idea is to use the recording of a period fight—even if only a few people are on stage, this effect is excellent with its explosions, gun-fire and sword-clashing sounds, along with the cast's bloodthirsty shouts.

The order that you use these notes depends on your production, but they do guarantee that everyone has good fight business to do. You may like one of the Pirates to swagger over to Busby's corner and thus Kenny enters when the Audience shouts. He waves a floppy sword, the blade being made of thick material painted silver, or thick silver foil in several layers. The Captain bravely draws his sword from the scabbard but the sword is only about one foot long. Robinson should remain swashbuckling throughout and his parries with Jack Boot and co. are serious, but don't let him meet and fight with Blackpatch as this moment comes in Act II. Some of the Sailors have wooden swords, the blades of wood being painted silver. Some of the pirates have prop rubber daggers. Polly can threaten with a mop as she duels with some pirate. Someone brandishes a loo brush.

Bill can swing across on a rope yelling "Jungle Fresh Peanuts". Someone can enter waving a sword at no-one in particular, thrashing at the air and making suitably loud Errol Flynn heroic noises and then exits the other side—he then re-enters and crosses, doing the same business again.

Robinson Crusoe

A traditional bit of pantomime business is a prop box camera held by the left hand. A pirate is encouraged to pose smiling into the camera (all in the middle of the fight!) and out of the lens shoots a boxing glove worked by the right hand. Each piece of comedy business should be done downstage or the audience won't notice it. The best business of all is Mrs Crusoe entering with a tin tray on which are a plastic cup and saucer. She charmingly offers the cup of tea to a somewhat surprised Pirate, who accepts. He takes the cup and saucer, drinks, and as he does so, Mrs Crusoe hits him on the head with the tin tray and he reacts, quickly puts the cup and saucer back on the proffered tray and staggers away. Mrs Crusoe continues this business with various Pirates all through the fight.

The Strange Shipwreck
During the thunder and lightning effects, suddenly drop the sails on each side of the mast by releasing them up in the flies, then they collapse inwards against the mast. The cut-out of the mast can sway—or even break in two by using a hinge pin. At the same time, the Demon Oylslick and his Minions are pulling rolls of black shiny plastic material over the top of the bulwarks, with assistance from offstage stagehands. They then spread these sheets and rolls of plastic across the stage as though the ship is sinking due to the black oil slick and this simple method when choreographed is effective, the movements being slow and "slimy".

The Fairy Detergenta's **bubbles**. On a small stage, the cast group at the one wing and blow bubbles on to the stage using the wire loops and soap bottles. If a large- or medium-sized production, you will need a bubble machine which is not expensive to hire from shops that sell props for discotheques, or apply to Theatre Projects Ltd, 10 Long Acre, London WC2.

The Dolphin Carriage is a simple truck about three feet square on castors, or hardboard cut-outs attached to a supermarket trolley (two supermarket trolleys lashed side by side for a bigger production) so that it looks like a sea green Roman chariot. Either Juveniles dressed as sea horses pull it on, or there are cut-outs of dolphins attached to the main carriage. If wing space is limited, draw the tabs after the comedy ballet, let the Demon and the Fairy challenge each other and then open the tabs on a non-moving cut-out of the sea chariot and dolphins, behind which Robinson can stand at the appropriate moment.

The cannibal **stewpot** with logs and flames under it is a hinged cut-out (about six feet long by four feet high) brought on by the cannibals and walking behind it, as though in it, are Mrs Crusoe and Kenny. Because it is hinged at the two ends, it can stand on the stage in front of them.

"Busy Bee". This is far and away the most famous of Victorian pantomime routines and still works well. The secret to it is that Bill, Ben and Mrs Crusoe never for one moment "send it up". Bill really does seriously want Ben to get the stupid poem about the Busy Bee right. It is best not to add any further jokes or the routine will become muddled. You may find at rehearsals that the main comic should not be Bill, but Ben or Mrs Crusoe—it is whoever has "the knack" of playing it best, and the parts are easily interchanged.

The Cannibal Attack. The heads of the cannibals that appear over the stockade fence can be cut-outs on sticks held up. If needed, one person can make three or four heads appear by holding up a T-shaped piece, with the cannibal heads and maybe shoulders attached along the T horizontal piece.

The Discovery Of The Treasure. There is an eight feet high cut-out representing a crumbled stone Buddha-like statue, and it is either part of the Ruined Temple cut-out, or it stands on its own. In professional productions of this pantomime the whole statue is pulled off into the wings to reveal the glittering pile of treasure behind, but I have seen amateur productions where the following idea works well. The cut-out is painted to look like a statue on a stone base or plinth, and this base is about four feet long by three feet high. This apparently solid base is merely a piece of hardboard that is pulled off into the wings when the magic word is called out. At once we see the glittering treasure which is in fact a box four feet by three feet, lined with crinkled gold and silver foil, containing jewellery, jars, urns, pots, etc, and behind these are electric bulbs. Over the bulbs place brightly coloured plastic or gelatine sheets so that the contents of what is in fact a large shallow box really do shine and glitter as this "discovery of the treasure" is the climax of the story.

The Cod Ballet (Mrs Crusoe and Kenny). You will have your own ideas but here is the basic routine. First, Kenny enters, poses with arms above his head and this causes his male classical ballet dancer black velvet tunic to ride up too far and, much embarrassed, he pulls it down at the front quickly. He then ushers in Mrs Crusoe in her tutu. She crosses as though on points, collects a fairly big red balloon from the wings, graciously hands it to Kenny but it is on an elastic and whizzes off into the wings. Both react. She collects a second one, holding it firmly with her fingers but as she graciously hands it to him she lets go of its nozzle and it also whizzes away, upwards and usually into the audience. You may find at rehearsal that this works better with a sausage balloon. She now collects a third and far larger balloon, and as she graciously hands it to Kenny he bursts it with a pin from his tunic. She angrily points to offstage so, muttering to himself, he exits.

While he has gone she does some turns on the spot, one leg held out, or attempts the splits. He re-enters with a beachball, not a balloon now, bounces it on the floor and she catches it and bounces it back. He now bounces it on to her bosom which she sticks out—percussion effects all through the routine—and now they put the large beachball between them, she facing upstage and he facing downstage. As she moves left, he moves right. When the ball is between their hands, they then move back "past each other" again, in the opposite direction to before. They then bow and curtsy as though this has been an amazing feat.

Now they face each other and he holds the beachball with his legs astride, and she does a very slow diving movement under the beachball and onwards, between his legs, where she gets stuck, the ball being in the hollow of her back and he is desperately trying to cope with her and the beachball, both of which are between his legs. She is on all fours and in the struggle her wig falls off "accidentally". They are both horrified and giggle. She puts it on again, looks out front and the wig is on backwards.

She now moves onwards through his legs, stands up (he still holding the ball) and both bow and curtsy. She then throws the beachball to offstage,

Robinson Crusoe

turns upstage and (facing her) he puts his hand round her waist. Then we see that he lowers his hand to her seat. She very firmly raises his hand with her hand to the correct area of her waist, pause, she changes her mind and lowers his hand to her seat area again.

She faces front. All through the routine either "Humoresque" or some well-known theme from Swan Lake or Sleeping Beauty, etc is played relentlessly over and over again as they embark on each phase of the routine. They start to dance across the stage, he behind her, hands around her waist. The music is building to the Grand Climax, the Magic Sea People enter, the end of the ballet is about to occur—but he can't lift her as she is too heavy! He tries several times, so then *she* lifts him, and with all the Chorus pointing towards them and posing, she exits staggering with *him* on *her* shoulders, or she holds his body horizontally as though he is a big fish. Applause, then the Chorus do the short serious ballet or dance routine, as in the script.

The Nautically Patriotic Finale. Let the Juveniles carry small Union Jacks which they wave at Curtain Call, and maybe some adults carry Union Jacks on poles, the Finale being a mixture of the patriotic and the comical.

Music. If you use the songs suggested, all of them should be played up tempo—the Gilbert and Sullivan and the traditional ones most especially so, as this is a boisterous pantomime and not an operetta.

There are so many comedy routines in this pantomime that you may find it best to keep the songs and dance routines short or the running time will far exceed the usual two and a half hours.

J.M.

FURNITURE AND PROPERTY LIST

Only essential properties and furniture are listed here. Please also see scenery and staging notes which appear after these plots

PROLOGUE

No properties required

ACT I

SCENE 1

On stage: Barrel. *In it:* creeper on nylon wire
Pub sign on scenery
Crates

Off stage: Yellow parrot in cage (chocolate eggs set in cage for Act II, Scene 6) **(Kenny)**
Large packet of "Polyfilla" **(Kenny)**
Cut-out of small boat **(Bill and Ben)**
2 large cardboard boxes **(Mrs Crusoe and Polly)**
Pen **(Captain)**

Personal: **Blackpatch:** gun, magic book
Robinson: catapult
Mrs Crusoe: coloured bucket containing toffees, scraggy piece of meat, chicken with two light bulbs attached (practical)
Old Jim: treasure map
Captain: signing-on papers

SCENE 2

Personal: **Blackpatch:** telescope
Captain: pound notes, pencil, carrier bag. *In it:* comics
Mrs Crusoe: paper, handbag
Polly: carrier bag. *In it:* sweets, pencils, etc
Kenny: two carrier bags. *In them:* sweets, pencils, etc. Eggs in one (actually ping pong balls)
Robinson: carrier bag. *In it:* sweets, toys, etc

SCENE 3

Set: Kitchen table. *On it:* bowl of dirty clothes, cloth, cake tins, bowls, red flower in pot, white flower in pot, tin of sardines, large pepper pot, large salt container, jug of water
Ship's lanterns (see production notes)
Kitchen stool
Stage cloth to catch water

Robinson Crusoe

Off stage: Fish (attached to nylon wire) on plate **(Bill)**

Personal: **Mrs Crusoe:** chef's hat

SCENE 4

Off stage: Lantern **(Blackpatch)**
Piece of hardboard **(Blackpatch)**

Personal: **Robinson:** chart, whistle on cord

SCENE 5

Off stage: Mops **(Mop crew)**
Rope **(Chorus)**
Bottles of rum **(Pirates)**
Daggers **(Pirates)**
Swords **(Pirates)**
Gun **(Pirates)**
Skull and crossbones flag **(Jack Boot)**

Personal: **Pirates:** black patches, earrings, etc
Robinson: sword
Kenny: whistle
Blackpatch: magic book, dagger in belt

SCENE 6

Personal: **Fairy:** wand

SCENE 7

No properties required

ACT II

SCENE 1

On stage: Carved totem pole
Palm tree
Tropical plants (optional)
Jungle drums (optional)

Set: White sole lining (in footlights)

Off stage: Water
Personal: **Robinson:** rifle, belt pouch, knife
Cannibals: spears, shields
Wotta Woppa: knife in belt
Friday: wooden bead necklace
Ben: handkerchief, flask of water

SCENE 2

Off stage: Cut-out of stewpot and flames

Personal: **Jack Boot:** gun
Blackpatch: very large safety pin
Cannibals: spears

SCENE 3

On stage: Stockade

Off stage: Egg **(Friday)**
Guns **(Bill** and **Polly)**
Plank **(Friday)**

Personal: **Captain:** telescope
Cannibals: spears
Wotta Woppa: spear
Blackpatch: pistol

SCENE 4

Personal: **Mrs Crusoe:** Handbag. *In it:* banana, mirror

SCENE 5

On stage: Crumbling statue with plinth containing treasure (see scenery and production notes)

Off stage: Tube and kitchen bowl **(Friday)**
Bottle of "Phyllosan" **(Blackpatch)**

Personal: **Robinson:** sword, chart
Blackpatch: sword, magic book

SCENE 6

No properties required

SCENE 7

Set: Union Jack flags everywhere

LIGHTING PLOT

Prologue

Cue 1	When ready *Light Captain in front of tabs (optional)*	(Page 1)

ACT I, Scene 1

To open: General outdoor lighting

Cue 2	As **Kenny** exits *Dim to leave green spot* DL	(Page 3)
Cue 3	As **Kenny** enters *Lights up to full*	(Page 3)
Cue 4	**Blackpatch:** "... harken to me!" *Green spot on barrel*	(Page 4)
Cue 5	After creeper disappears *Lights revert to normal*	(Page 4)
Cue 6	After Song 2 *Lights darken. Spot on Blackpatch*	(Page 6)
Cue 7	**Blackpatch** exits *Cut out spot*	(Page 8)
Cue 8	**Old Jim:** "... something for 'ee, Robinson ..." *Fade to spot on Old Jim and Robinson*	(Page 12)
Cue 9	As **Blackpatch** enters *Green spot on Blackpatch*	(Page 12)
Cue 10	**Blackpatch** exits *Cut spot*	(Page 12)
Cue 11	As **Robinson** waves at end of Song 5 *Black-out*	(Page 14)

ACT I, Scene 2

To open: Dim lighting

Cue 12	At end of Song 6 *Black-out*	(Page 19)

ACT I, Scene 3

To open: General lighting

Cue 13	**Mrs Crusoe, Bill, Ben:** "Help! No!" *Black-out*	(Page 23)

ACT I, Scene 4

To open: Dim lighting

No cues

ACT I, Scene 5

To open: General lighting

Cue 14	After mop crew exit *Dim lights*	(Page 30)
Cue 15	After Pirate fight *Revert to general lighting*	(Page 33)
Cue 16	**Blackpatch:** "... and the slime you creep ..." *Flicker, then dim lights*	(Page 34)
Cue 17	**Blackpatch:** "... depths of the slimy sea. Ha, ha, ha!" *Fade to spot on Blackpatch and Oylslick*	(Page 35)

ACT I, Scene 6

To open: Continuous with Scene 5

No cues

ACT I, Scene 7

To open: Underwater lighting

No cues

ACT II, Scene 1

To open: Exterior lighting

Cue 18	**Ben** squirts **Bill**, Vaudeville music *Black-out*	(Page 47)

ACT II, Scene 2

To open: Exterior lighting

Cue 19	**Cannibals** chase **Mrs Crusoe** and **Kenny** *Black-out*	(Page 52)

ACT II, Scene 3

To open: Exterior lighting

Cue 20	**Cannibals** exit *Black-out*	(Page 57)

ACT II, Scene 4

To open: Exterior lighting

Cue 21	**Mrs Crusoe** exits *Black-out*	(Page 60)

ACT II, SCENE 5

To open: Exterior lighting

Cue 22	**All** shout: "Jackanory!" (2nd time) *Lights flicker*	(Page 64)
Cue 23	(Optional: if **Wotta Woppa** and **Blackpatch** scene played before tabs) *Light front of tabs only*	(Page 64)
Cue 24	After Song 16 *Black-out*	(Page 65)

ACT II, SCENE 6

To open: Exterior lighting

No cues

ACT II, SCENE 7

To open: Exterior lighting

No cues

EFFECTS PLOT

Please note that although Fanfares are included, other "musical" cues (roll on drums, swanee whistle, etc) are not listed here as it is assumed that the orchestra will perform them on visual cues

PROLOGUE

Cue 1	**Prologue:** "His name?" *Fanfare*	(Page 1)

ACT I

Cue 2	**Ben:** "... and the weather is—". *Water sloshed in Ben's face*	(Page 20)
Cue 3	**Ben:** "... tidal wave had hit me and—". *Water sloshed in Ben's face*	(Page 20)
Cue 4	**Mrs Crusoe:** "... they call accident prone." *Lantern crashes on her head and goes up again*	(Page 20)
Cue 5	**Mrs Crusoe:** "... some flour as quick as you can." *Talcum powder effect*	(Page 21)
Cue 6	**Ben:** "... covered in flour and ..." *Water comes through porthole*	(Page 21)
Cue 7	**Mrs Crusoe:** "... they call *accident prone* and—" *Lantern hits her head and goes up again*	(Page 21)
Cue 8	**Mrs Crusoe:** "... they call *accident prone!*" *Three lanterns hit all three on stage*	(Page 23)
Cue 9	At beginning of Song 9 *Fanfare*	(Page 31)
Cue 10	**Blackpatch:** "BEHOLD—DEMON OYLSLICK!" *Gurgling sounds*	(Page 35)
Cue 11	As ship is swamped in oil *Gurgling and sucking sounds*	(Page 35)
Cue 12	**Fairy:** "... Robinson get to *dry* land!" *Fanfare*	(Page 39)

ACT II

NB: Drumbeats in Act II should be performed live by the Cannibals, either on stage or in the wings

Cue 13	**Robinson** aims gun *Shot fired in wings*	(Page 41)
Cue 14	**Kenny:** "... thousands of miles away *Fanfare*	(Page 56)
Cue 15	**Kenny:** "Whoever heard of grunting gorillas?" *Ug-ug noises*	(Page 58)
Cue 16	**Bill:** "... grunting gorillas just then!" *Ug-ug noises*	(Page 58)
Cue 17	**Jack Boot** staggers off *Crash off*	(Page 61)
Cue 18	**All** shout "Jackanory" (2nd time) *Thunder and fanfare*	(Page 64)
Cue 19	**Nelson** and **Robinson** shake hands *Fanfare*	(Page 64)

MADE AND PRINTED IN GREAT BRITAIN BY
LATIMER TREND & COMPANY LTD PLYMOUTH
MADE IN ENGLAND